Henrietta Latham Dwight

The Golden Age Cook Book

Henrietta Latham Dwight

The Golden Age Cook Book

ISBN/EAN: 9783744788663

Printed in Europe, USA, Canada, Australia, Japan

Cover: Foto ©Andreas Hilbeck / pixelio.de

More available books at **www.hansebooks.com**

THE

GOLDEN AGE

COOK BOOK.

❧ ❧ ❧ ❧

HENRIETTA LATHAM DWIGHT

NEW YORK:
THE ALLIANCE PUBLISHING COMPANY,
"LIFE" BUILDING,
1898.

PRESS OF THE PLIMPTON MFG. CO.,
HARTFORD, CONN.

Dedication.

TO ALL WHO ARE STRIVING TO FOLLOW THE GOLDEN
RULE, "TO DO UNTO OTHERS AS THEY WOULD
HAVE OTHERS DO UNTO THEM," AND THUS
EXPRESS IN THEIR EVERY-DAY LIFE
THE CHRIST IDEAL, WRITTEN
WITHIN, IN THEIR OWN
SOULS, THIS BOOK
IS

Affectionately Inscribed.

And God said, Behold, I have given you every herb bearing seed, which is upon the face of all the earth, and every tree, in the which is the fruit of a tree yielding seed; to you it shall be for meat. And to every beast of the earth, and to every fowl of the air, and to every thing that creepeth upon the earth, wherein there is life, I have given every green herb for meat: and it was so.—Genesis i., 29, 30.

Thou shalt not kill.—Exodus xx., 13.

For that which befalleth the sons of men befalleth beasts; even one thing befalleth them: as the one dieth, so dieth the other; yea, they have all one breath; so that a man hath no pre-eminence above a beast: for all is vanity. All go unto one place; all are of the dust, and all turn to dust again. Who knoweth the spirit of man that goeth upward, and the spirit of the beast that goeth downward to the earth?—Ecclesiastes iii., 19, 20, 21.

He that killeth an ox is as if he slew a man.—Isaiah lxvi., 3.

Then said Daniel to Melzar [the steward], whom the prince of the eunuchs had set over Daniel, Hananiah, Mishael, and Azariah: Prove thy servants, I beseech thee, ten days; and let them give us pulse to eat, and water to drink. Then let our countenances be looked upon before thee, and the countenance of the children that eat of the portion of the king's meat: and as thou seest, deal with thy servants. So he consented to them in this matter, and proved them ten days. And at the end of ten days their countenances appeared fairer and fatter in flesh than all the children which did eat the portion of the king's meat.—Daniel i., 11 to 17.

Preface.

I SEND this little book out into the world, first, to aid those who, having decided to adopt a bloodless diet, are still asking how they can be nourished without flesh; second, in the hope of gaining something further to protect " the speechless ones " who, having come down through the centuries under " the dominion of man," have in their eyes the mute, appealing look of the helpless and oppressed. Their eloquent silence should not ask our sympathy and aid in vain; they have a right, as our humble brothers, to our loving care and protection, and to demand justice and pity at our hands; and, as a part of the One Life, to—

> " life, which all can take but none can give :
> Life, which all creatures love and strive to keep :
> Wonderful, dear, and pleasant unto each,
> Even to the meanest; yea, a boon to all
> Where pity is, for pity makes the world
> Soft to the weak and noble for the strong.
> Unto the dumb lips of the flock he lent
> Sad, pleading words, showing how man, who prays
> For mercy to the gods, is merciless,
> Being as god to those; albeit all life
> Is linked and kin, and what we slay have given
> Meek tribute of their milk and wool, and set
> Fast trust upon the hands which murder them."

If the cruelty and injustice to animals are nothing to us, we have still another argument to offer—the brutalization of the men who slaughter that we may eat flesh. Mrs. Besant, in " Why I Am a Food Reformer," says:

" Lately I have been in the city of Chicago—one of the greatest slaughter-houses of the world—where the slaughter-men, who are employed from early morn till late at night in the killing of thousands of these hapless creatures, are made a class *practically apart from their fellow-men;* they are marked out by the police *as the most dangerous part of the community;* amongst them are committed most crimes of violence, and the most ready use of the knife is found. One day I was speaking to an authority on this subject, and I asked him how it was that he knew so decidedly that most of the murders and the crimes with the knife were perpetrated by that particular class of men, and his answer was suggestive, although horrible. He said: 'There is a peculiar turn of the knife which men learn to use in the slaughter-house, for, as the living creatures are brought to them by machinery, these men slit their throats as they pass by. That twist of the wrist is the characteristic of most crimes with the knife committed amongst our Chicago population.' That struck me at once as both a horrible and significant fact. *What right have people to condemn other men to a trade that makes them so readily take to the knife in anger; which marks them out as specially brutalized—brutes amongst their fellow-men?* Being constantly in the sight and the smell of blood, their whole nature is coarsened; accustomed to kill thousands of creatures, they lose all sense of reverence for sentient life, they grow indifferent to the suffering they continually see around them ; accustomed to inflict pain, they grow callous to the sight of pain ; accustomed to kill swiftly, and sometimes not even waiting until the creature is dead before the skin is stripped from it, their nerves become coarsened, hardened, and brutalized, and they are less men as men because they are slaughterers of animals. *And everyone who eats flesh meat has part in that brutalization ; everyone who uses what they provide is guilty of this degradation of his fellow-men.*

" If I may not appeal to you in the name of the animals— if under mistaken views you regard animals as not sharing *your kind of life*—then I appeal to you in the name of *human brotherhood,* and remind you of your duty to your fellow-men, your duty to your nation, which must be built up partly of the children of those who slaughter--who physically inherit the very signs of this brutalizing occupation. I ask you to recognize your duty as men and women who should *raise* the Race, not

6

degrade it; who should try to make it *divine*, not *brutal*; who should try to make it *pure*, not *foul*; and therefore, in the name of Human Brotherhood, I appeal to you to leave your own tables free from the stain of blood and your consciences free from the degradation of your fellow-men."

That flesh-eating is not necessary to the perfect health of man is attested by many scientists. The following testimonies from some very prominent physiologists and anatomists may prove interesting:

Sir Charles Bell, F. R. S.: "It is, I think, not going too far to say that every fact connected with the human organization goes to prove that man was originally formed a frugivorous animal. This opinion is principally derived from the formation of his teeth and digestive organs, as well as from the character of his skin and the general structure of his limbs."

Sylvester Graham, M. D.: "Comparative anatomy proves that man is naturally a frugivorous animal, formed to subsist upon fruits, seeds, and farinaceous vegetables."

Professor Wm. Lawrence, F. R. S.: "The teeth of man have not the slightest resemblance to those of carnivorous animals; and, whether we consider the teeth, jaws, or digestive organs, the human structure closely resembles that of the frugivorous animals."

Dr. Jozef Drzewiecki: "There is no doubt that fruit and vegetable food purifies the blood, while meat inflames and is the source of many diseases, which are the punishment for breaking the natural law and command."

Professor Vogt: "The vegetarian diet is the most beneficial and agreeable to our organs, as it contains the greatest amount of carbon hydrates and the best proportion of albumen."

Sir Henry Thompson, M. D., F. R. C. S.: "It is a vulgar error to regard meat in any form as necessary to life. All that is necessary to the human body can be supplied by the vegetable kingdom. . . . The vegetarian can extract from his food all the principles necessary for the growth and support of the body, as well as for the production of heat and force. It must

7

be admitted as a fact beyond all question that some persons are stronger and more healthy who live on that food. I know how much of the prevailing meat diet is not merely a wasteful extravagance, but a source of serious evil to the consumer."

The following special cablegram from London to the New York "Sun," July 3d, 1898, contains a practical illustration of the superiority of a vegetable diet:

"The vegetarians are making a great ado over the triumph of their theory in the long-distance test of walking endurance, seventy miles, in Germany, this week. The twenty-two starters included eight vegetarians. The distance had to be covered within eighteen hours. The first six to arrive were vegetarians, the first finishing in $14\frac{1}{4}$ hours, the second in $14\frac{1}{2}$, the third in $15\frac{1}{2}$, the fourth in 16, the fifth in $16\frac{1}{2}$, and the sixth in $17\frac{1}{2}$. The last two vegetarians missed their way and walked five miles more. All reached the goal in splendid condition. Not till one hour after the last vegetarian did the first meat-eater appear, completely exhausted. He was the only one. Others dropped off after thirty-five miles."

There is no question of the great economy of vegetarianism. Dr. Alcott, in "Arguments for Vegetarianism," says:

"Twenty-two acres of land are needed to sustain one man on fresh meat. Under wheat that land will feed forty-two people; under oats, eighty-eight; under potatoes, maize, or rice, one hundred and seventy-six; under the banana, over six thousand. The crowded nations of the future must abandon flesh-eating for a diet that will feed more than tenfold people by the same soil, expense and labor. How rich men will be when they cease to toil for flesh-meat, alcohol, drugs, sickness, and war!"

"Suffer the ox to plough, and impute his death to age and Nature's hand.
Let the sheep continue to yield us sheltering wool, and the goats the produce of their loaded udders.
Banish from among you nets and snares and painful artifices,
Conspire no longer against the birds, nor scare the meek deer, nor hide with fraud the crooked hook; . . . .
But let your mouths be empty of blood, and satisfied with pure and natural repasts."*

* Imputed to Pythagoras.

COMPARATIVE TABLES

OF

Vegetable and Animal

FOODS.

	Nitrogenous Matter.	Hydrocarbonate Matter.	Saline Matter.	Water.
Lean beef...	19.3	3.6	5.1	72.0
Fat beef............................	14.8	29.8	4.4	51.0
Lean mutton.....................	18.3	4.9	4.8	72.0
Fat mutton.......................	12.4	31.1	3.5	53.0
Veal	16.5	15.8	4.7	63.0
Fat pork..........................	9.8	48.9	2.3	39.0
Dried ham........................	8.8	73.3	2.9	15.0
Tripe...............................	13.2	16.4	2.4	68.0
White fish........................	18.1	2.9	1.0	78.0
Red fish (salmon)..............	16.1	5.5	1.4	77.0
Oysters............................	14.010	1.515	2.695	80.385
Mussels..........	11.72	2.42	2.73	75.74
White of egg.....................	20.4	......	1.6	78.0
Yolk of egg.......................	16.0	30.7	1.3	52.0
Cow's milk (lactin)	4.1	3.9	0.8	86.0
Cream.............................	2.7	26.7	1.8	66.0
Butter.............................		83.0	2.0	15.0
Gruyere cheese..................	31.5	24.0	3.0	40.0
Roquefort........................	26.52	30.14	5.07	34.55
Dutch..............................	29.43	27.54		36.10
Chester............................	25.99	26.34	4.16	35.92
Parmesan........................	44.08	15.95	5.72	27.56
Cheddar..........................	28.4	31.1	4.5	36.0

IN 100 PARTS.

	Carbo-hydrates.	Nitrog-enous Matter.	Hydro-carbonate Matter.	Saline Matter.	Water.
Beans	55.86	30.8	2.0	3.65	8.40
White haricots	55.7	25.5	2.8	3.2	9.9
Dried peas	58.7	23 8	2.1	2.1	8.3
Lentils	56.0	25.2	2.6	2.3	11.5
Potatoes	21.9	2.50	0.11	1.26	74.0
Black truffles	16.0	8.775	0.560	2.070	72.0
Mushrooms	3.0	4.680	0.396	0.458	91.010
Carrots	14.5	1.3	0.2	1.0	83.0
Sea-kale	2.8	2.4	......	(?) 3.0	93.3
Turnips	7.2	1.1	......	0.6	91.0
Cabbage	5.8	2.0	0.5	0.7	91.0
Garden beet	13.5	.4		(?) 1.0	82.2
Tomato	6.0	1.4	......	(?) .8	89.8
Sweet potato	26.25	1.50	0.30	2.60	67.50
Water-cress	3.2	1.7	......	(?) .7	93.1
Arrowroot	82.0	......	......	......	18.0
Dry southern wheat.	67.112	22.75	2.61	3.02	......
Dry common wheat..	77.05	15.25	1.95	2.75	......
Oat-meal	63.8	12.6	5.6	3.0	15.0
Barley-meal	74.3	6.3	2.4	2.0	15.0
Rye-meal	73.2	8.0	2.0	1.8	15.0
Dry maize	71.55	12.50	8.80	1.25	......
Dry rice	89.65	7.55	0.80	0.90	......
Buckwheat	64.90	13.10	3.0	2.50	13.0
Quinoa-meal	56.80	20.0	5.0	(?) 1.0	15.0
Dhoorra-meal	74.0	9.0	2.6	2.3	......
Dried figs	65.9	6.1	0.9	2.3	17.5
Dates	65.3	6.6	0.2	1.6	20.8
Bananas	(?)19.0	4.820	0.632	0.791	73.900
Walnuts (peeled)	8.9	12.5	31.6	(?) 1.7	44.5
Filberts	11.1	8.4	28.5	(?) 1.5	48.0
Ground-nuts (peeled)	11.7	24.5	50.0	(?) 1.8	7.5
Cocoa-nut	8.1	5.5	35.9	(?) 1.0	46.6
Fresh chestnuts (peeled)	42.7	3.0	2.5	(?) 1.8	49.2
Locust bean	67.9	7.1	1.1	(?) 2.9	14.6
Cocoa-nibs) Chocolate)	11.10	21.20	50.0	3.0	12.0

The analyses are those of Fresenius, Letheby, Pavy, Church, and others.
From " The Perfect Way in Diet."

"O Golden Age, whose light is of the dawn,
And not of sunset, forward, not behind,
Flood the new heavens and earth, and with thee bring
All the old virtues, whatsoever things
Are pure and honest and of good repute,
But add thereto whatever bard has sung
Or seer has told of when in trance or dream
They saw the Happy Isles of prophecy!
Let Justice hold her scale, and Truth divide
Between the right and wrong; but give the heart
The freedom of its fair inheritance."

—WHITTIER.

12

Bread, Biscuit, and Rolls.

BEATEN BISCUIT.—No. 1.

One quart of flour, two teaspoonfuls of baking powder sifted with the flour, a quarter of a teaspoonful of salt, a large heaping tablespoonful of butter, milk enough to make a stiff dough. Beat with a rolling pin or in a biscuit-beater for ten or fifteen minutes until the dough blisters. Roll out about half an inch thick or less, prick well with a fork and bake in a quick oven.

BEATEN BISCUIT.—No. 2.

Two quarts of flour, three ounces of butter, a little salt and enough water to make a stiff dough. Beat with a rolling pin or in a biscuit-beater twenty minutes until the dough blisters or snaps. Roll out about half an inch thick, prick well with a fork and bake in a quick oven. This dough rolled very thin, cut with a large cutter, pricked well and baked in a quick oven makes delicious wafers to serve with tea or chocolate.

BAKING-POWDER BISCUIT.

One quart of sifted flour, three-quarters of a cup of butter, two heaping teaspoonfuls of baking powder, one teaspoonful of salt, enough milk to make a soft dough. Do not handle any more than is necessary. Roll thin, cut in small biscuits, prick with a fork and bake in a quick oven.

CREAM BISCUIT.

One quart of flour sifted, two rounded teaspoonfuls of Cleveland's baking powder, two cupfuls of

13

cream and a little salt. Mix, roll out about a quarter of an inch thick, cut with a small biscuit-cutter, prick with a fork and bake fifteen or twenty minutes in a quick oven.

FRENCH ROLLS.

Two quarts of sifted flour, a pint of warm milk, half a cup of butter melted in the milk, a quarter of a cup of sugar, three or four eggs beaten light, a little salt, a half cake of compressed yeast, dissolved in a little warm milk. Make a batter of the milk and flour, add the eggs and sugar, beat hard for fifteen minutes. Cover the pan and set to rise, over night if for luncheon, in the morning if for tea. Knead well, but do not add any more flour. Make them into shape and let them rise again until light. Bake about fifteen minutes in a quick oven. For buns add cinnamon. Sift the flour before measuring, and measure lightly.

RAISED FINGER-ROLLS.

Half a pint of milk, half a pint of water, one-third of a compressed yeast cake, one teaspoonful of sugar, two teaspoonfuls of butter, one teaspoonful of salt. Dissolve the yeast cake in a little tepid water, mix as usual, make into a soft dough at night, bake for breakfast or luncheon.

WINDSOR ROLLS.

Melt half a cup of butter in three-quarters of a pint of warm milk, dissolve one cake of compressed yeast in a little tepid milk, stir together and add a teaspoonful of salt and enough flour to make like bread dough, set to rise in a warm place. It will rise in about two hours. Roll out the dough, using as little flour as possible to keep it from sticking, and cut with a biscuit-cutter, or mould with the hands into rolls, put them in pans, and set on the shelf over the range to rise about ten or fifteen minutes. Bake fifteen or twenty minutes.

ELIZABETTI ROLLS.

One cup of sweet milk, half a yeast cake, an even tablespoonful of butter, two teaspoonfuls of sugar, and one of salt, and flour enough to make as stiff as bread dough. Scald the milk and melt the butter in it, when lukewarm dissolve the yeast cake, sugar and salt and stir the flour in until as thick as bread dough. Set to rise over night. In the morning roll thin, cut with a biscuit-cutter, put a tiny lump of butter on each biscuit, fold in half, set to rise again, and when light bake about twenty minutes in a moderate oven. This quantity will make twenty-four rolls.

RYE ROLLS.

Take in the morning from rye bread dough one cupful, add to it a tablespoonful of Porto Rico molasses, one tablespoonful of sour cream, one even tablespoonful of butter. Bake in cups, half fill them, set in a warm place to rise for three-quarters of an hour, and bake fifteen minutes. This quantity will make eight.

GLUTEN ROLLS.

Three cups of kernel flour, two even tablespoonfuls of baking powder, half a teaspoonful of salt, two cups of milk. Mix the flour, salt and baking powder together, then stir in the milk, beat well. If baked in iron roll pans heat them well, brush with butter; if granite ware, only grease them. This quantity will make sixteen rolls. Bake from twenty to twenty-five minutes.

PARKER HOUSE ROLLS.

Sift two cups of flour with half a teaspoonful of salt and one teaspoonful of sugar, then add a cup of tepid water in which a cake of compressed yeast has been dissolved, two tablespoonfuls of melted butter; when mixed break in one egg and add flour enough to make a soft dough. Knead well, beating the dough upon the board. Set to rise in a warm place, when light knead again, adding only enough flour to keep from sticking to the board, roll out about half an inch thick, cut with a biscuit-cutter, brush with melted butter, fold in half and set to rise again. These rolls can be set at noon if for tea, or in the morning if for luncheon, or they can be made up at night for breakfast, when use only half a yeast cake. This dough can be moulded into small, oblong rolls for afternoon teas.

BOSTON BROWN BREAD.

One cup of yellow corn meal, one cup and a half of Graham flour, an even teaspoonful of salt, an even teaspoonful of soda, two cups of sour milk, half a cup of Porto Rico molasses, and butter the size of a large walnut. Sift the corn meal and soda together, add the Graham flour and salt, then the milk and molasses, melt the butter and stir in at the last. Butter a brown bread mould, pour in the mixture, steam for three hours, keep the water steadily boiling, remove the cover of the mould, and bake twenty minutes in the oven to form a crust.

BOSTON BROWN BREAD WITH RAISINS.

Follow the preceding recipe, adding a cup of raisins stoned and slightly chopped. Very nice for nut sandwiches and stewed bread.

BOSTON BROWN BREAD STEWED.

Cut the bread into dice, and when the milk boils add the bread and stew gently fifteen minutes. The proportion is about a cup of milk to one of bread.

GRAHAM BREAD.

Half a pint of milk, half a pint of water, a pint and a half of white flour, an even teaspoonful of salt, half a yeast cake dissolved in tepid water. Scald the milk and add the half pint of boiling water, set away to cool. Put the flour into the bread pan, add milk and water when lukewarm and the dissolved yeast; beat well. In the morning add half a cup of Porto Rico molasses and Graham flour enough to knead well, let it rise for three hours, knead again, make into loaves and set in a warm place to rise. When light bake in a moderate oven nearly an hour.

RYE BREAD.

Dissolve half a yeast cake, two heaping teaspoonfuls of sugar and one of salt in a cup and a third of tepid water, then stir into it a pint of white flour, and when smooth add enough rye flour to make a dough rather stiffer than that of white bread. Knead thoroughly about fifteen minutes and set to rise. In the morning make into a loaf and put in a crusty bread pan.

QUICK WHITE BREAD.

Three pints of flour, an even teaspoonful of salt, two cakes of compressed yeast dissolved in tepid water and enough milk to make a soft dough. Set in the morning,—it will require about an hour and a half to rise, and, after making into loaves, about ten minutes.

DATE BREAD.

Break the dates apart, wash and drain them in a colander, shake them well, set in a warm place to dry. Stone and chop enough to make a cupful, and knead into a loaf of white bread just before setting to rise for the last time.

COFFEE BREAD.—No. 1.

One pound of flour, two eggs, six tablespoonfuls of melted butter, six ounces of sugar, a teaspoonful of soda, a teaspoonful of cream of tartar mixed dry in the flour, and one cup and a half of milk. Beat the butter and sugar together, add the eggs well beaten, a few grains of cardamom, half a cupful of raisins seeded, and a tablespoonful of citron cut fine, if liked, then add the milk and flour. Bake in crusty bread pans or shallow pans, as convenient.

COFFEE BREAD.—No. 2.

Half a pound of flour, one egg, two teaspoonfuls of sugar, a small pinch of salt, three tablespoonfuls of melted butter, three-quarters of a cup of milk, one even teaspoonful of soda, two scant teaspoonfuls of cream of tartar. Mix and bake in a crusty bread pan in a good oven, not too quick, from twenty to twenty-five minutes.

NORWEGIAN ROLLS.

Two pounds and a half of flour, a pint and a half of milk, half a pound of butter, six ounces of sugar, one even teaspoonful of cardamom seeds pounded fine, and one cake of compressed yeast. Melt the butter in the milk, mix the sugar, flour and cardamom together and stir the butter and milk into it with the yeast cake dissolved in a little milk, mix thoroughly and set to rise. When it is nicely raised, roll out the dough and cut with a biscuit-cutter, put in pans to rise again,—if they can be raised over steam it is better. When light bake in a quick oven. If zwieback are wanted, cut the biscuit in half when cold and set them in the oven to brown. If wanted very nice, brush each half over with white of egg and sprinkle with sugar and chopped almonds. The cardamom seed may be omitted if not liked.

RICE MUFFINS.

Boil a scant half cup of rice in salted water half an hour, drain well, and measure out four heaping tablespoonfuls of it into a mixing bowl. Stir into it while hot a heaping tablespoonful of butter. Beat one egg light, add to the rice and butter with a little salt, sift half a pint of flour with half a teaspoonful of baking powder, and stir in alternately with half a pint of milk. Pour the mixture into muffin rings or gem pans, which must be heated thoroughly and well buttered. Bake about twenty minutes.

LAPLANDS.

Half a pint of flour, half a pint of rich milk, a quarter of a teaspoonful of salt, three eggs beaten separately and very light. Mix the flour, salt and milk together, then the yolks of eggs, and lastly the whites of eggs beaten to a stiff froth. Have a gem pan very hot, butter well and fill with the batter and bake in a quick oven twelve to fifteen minutes. This quantity will make fourteen gems.

ENGLISH MUFFINS.

Half a pint of hot milk, half a pint of hot water, half a yeast cake, an even teaspoonful of salt and one of sugar, and about a pound and a half of white flour. Dissolve the yeast cake in a little tepid water and add to the batter when lukewarm. The milk and water mixed must be stirred into the flour while hot. Beat the batter very hard, ten or fifteen minutes; it should be a soft dough. Set to rise over night. Flour the board well, drop the dough in large spoonfuls in the flour, flatten with the hands and form into shape. Let them rise on the board in a warm place, and when light bake on a griddle, heated only half as hot as for griddle cakes. Flour the muffins and bake slowly on one side six minutes;

then turn and bake the same on the other side. They are very nice split and toasted and buttered immediately and put together again.

GRAHAM POPOVERS.

Beat three eggs very light, and add to them one tablespoonful of sugar, one pint of milk, a saltspoonful of salt. Put in a mixing bowl half a pint each of Graham and white flour, stir the eggs and milk gradually into this and beat until perfectly smooth. Then add one tablespoonful of melted butter and beat again for some minutes. Brush the cups over with melted butter; if they are of iron heat them, half fill with the batter and bake in a quick oven fifty minutes at least.

GRAHAM GEMS.

To one quart of sweet milk, four cups of Graham flour, a teaspoonful of salt. Stir together and beat well, the longer the better. Have the gem pans very hot, brush well with butter, half fill them with the batter and bake thirty-five minutes.

GEMS OF KERNEL (Middlings) AND WHITE FLOUR.

Two cups of kernel flour, two cups of white flour, four cups of milk or two of milk and two of water, one egg, a little salt, a heaping teaspoonful of sugar, two teaspoonfuls of baking powder, two large tablespoonfuls of melted butter. Beat the egg very light in a bowl, add the sugar and salt, the milk and butter, sift the flour together and beat the batter hard for a few minutes. Have the iron gem pans very hot, butter and fill, and bake them in a good, quick oven not less than thirty-five minutes.

GEMS OF RYE MEAL.

Mix together three-quarters of a cup of rye meal and a quarter of a cup of white flour and a saltspoonful of salt. Beat two egg yolks and stir into it a cup of sweet milk and one tablespoonful of granulated sugar, add this to the rye meal and flour, beat hard, then add the whites of two eggs beaten to a stiff froth. Heat the iron gem pans, brush with butter and bake thirty-five to forty minutes.

CORN BATTER BREAD.

Pour a pint of boiling milk over four heaping tablespoonfuls of yellow corn meal, add a heaping teaspoonful of butter, a heaping teaspoonful of sugar, and a little salt. Beat the yolks of three eggs to a cream and add to the batter, then the whites of three eggs beaten to a stiff froth. Butter a pudding dish, turn the mixture into it and bake from twenty-five to thirty minutes. Serve immediately in the dish in which it is baked.

CORN BREAD.

Put half a pint of yellow corn meal in a mixing bowl, pour over it one pint of rich, sweet milk. When cold add two tablespoonfuls of melted butter, half a teaspoonful of salt, one teaspoonful of sugar and four eggs beaten separately, the whites beaten to a stiff froth and added at the last. Pour into a well-buttered shallow pan and bake about half an hour in a good oven.

CORN GRIDDLE CAKES.

One cup of yellow corn meal in a mixing bowl, pour over it three cups of boiling milk. When cold add two tablespoonfuls of melted butter, two teaspoonfuls of sugar, one teaspoonful of salt. Sift one teaspoonful of cream of tartar and half a teaspoonful of soda with half a cup of white flour, add to the batter and at the last mix in two well-beaten eggs.

WHITE BREAD GRIDDLE CAKES.

Chop as much stale bread as will measure two cupfuls, put it into a bowl and pour over it a cupful of sweet, rich milk, let it soak for an hour. When ready to bake the cakes, mash the bread in the milk with a wooden spoon, add a heaping teaspoonful of sugar, a teaspoonful of salt, two tablespoonfuls of melted butter, two well-beaten eggs, sift into the mixture a cupful of white flour and an even teaspoonful of soda, stir well together, then add a cupful of sour milk and bake on a griddle.

BOSTON BROWN BREAD GRIDDLE CAKES.

Crumble enough Boston brown bread to make two cupfuls, pour over it a cup of sweet milk, soak an hour. Then mash fine in the milk, add two tablespoonfuls of melted butter, an even teaspoonful of salt, two well-beaten eggs, and sift into the mixture a cupful of white flour and a heaping teaspoonful of baking powder, beat well; then add a scant half cup of milk and bake as other griddle cakes.

WAFFLES.

Put a quart of milk to warm, melt a quarter of a pound of butter in it and stir in a teaspoonful of salt. When cold add a pint of sifted flour, four eggs, the whites and yolks beaten separately, and just before baking stir in two teaspoonfuls of baking powder.

EPICUREAN ROLLS.

Boil several potatoes and put them through a vegetable press or else grate them, measure one cupful, one tablespoonful of sugar, half a yeast cake dissolved in half a cup of tepid water, half a pint of milk, half a cup of butter, one egg beaten separately, half a teaspoonful of salt, and flour enough to make a soft dough. Set to rise at night. Pour a third of a cup of boiling water over the potato, salt and sugar. Beat smooth, and when tepid add the yeast, cover and set away to rise. In the morning bring the milk to a boil, and melt the butter in it; when cool enough add the beaten yolk and stir all into the potato sponge, beat the white of egg to a stiff froth and add to the other ingredients, with flour enough to make a soft dough; knead well and let it rise again; when very light roll out about half an inch thick, cut with a round biscuit-cutter, prick them with a fork, put in pans for a short time to rise and bake from fifteen to twenty minutes. The most delicate and delicious of rolls.

BREAD FROM RUMMER FLOUR.

Two quarts of improved Graham flour, half a pint of boiling water, half a pint of lukewarm water, one-fourth of a yeast cake dissolved in half a pint of lukewarm water, one tablespoonful of granulated sugar added when kneading the dough, one tea-spoonful of salt. Put the salt in the flour, make a hole, pour in the boiling water, then the lukewarm water, and last the yeast. Knead well at night at least fifteen minutes, set to rise. In the morning mould into loaves, let it rise until very light and bake until well done.

BISCUITS OF KERNEL OR GRAHAM FLOUR.

Follow the recipe for baking powder biscuits, using kernel or Graham flour instead of white flour. If Graham is used sift twice before adding the baking powder. Roll thin, cut with a biscuit-cutter, prick with a fork and bake in a quick oven.

Eggs.

TO SOFT BOIL EGGS.

Cover the eggs with cold water in a saucepan, place over the fire, and when the water comes to the boiling point the eggs are perfectly cooked; remove at once and serve.

TO HARD BOIL EGGS.

Put the eggs in boiling water and boil hard for ten minutes, set them where they will boil gently for ten minutes more, then remove from the fire. Eggs boiled in this way will be tender and digestible.

EGGS À LA CRÈME.

Boil twelve eggs fifteen minutes. Line a dish with very thin slices of bread and fill with layer of eggs cut in slices, strewing them with a little grated bread, pepper and salt; rub a quarter of a pound of butter with two tablespoonfuls of flour, put it in a saucepan with a tablespoonful of chopped parsley, a little onion grated, salt, pepper and half a pint of milk or cream; when hot pour over the eggs; cover the top with grated bread crumbs and put it in the oven, let it heat thoroughly and brown.

EGGS AU GRATIN.

Boil twelve eggs hard, shell and cut them in slices and lay them in a deep dish in close circular rows; make a sauce of a tablespoonful of butter, the yolks of four eggs, a little grated cheese, and half a pint of milk; stir this over the fire until it thickens, pour it over the eggs, strew some bread crumbs on top and bake for ten minutes.

24

NUN'S TOAST.

Cut four or five hard boiled eggs into thin slices; put a piece of butter half the size of an egg in a saucepan, and when it begins to bubble add a teaspoonful of grated onion; let it cook a little without taking color, then stir in a teaspoonful of flour and a cupful of milk and stir until smooth; add pepper and salt to taste, then put in the slices of egg and let them get hot. Have ready some neatly trimmed slices of buttered toast, pour the mixture over them and serve at once.

EGGS À LA MAÎTRE D'HÔTEL.

One-quarter of a pound of fresh butter, half a pint of milk, one tablespoonful of flour, one tablespoonful of minced parsley, half a teaspoonful of onion juice, one-fourth of a teaspoonful of white pepper, salt to taste, the juice of half a lemon, and eight hard boiled eggs. Stir the flour and half of the butter in a saucepan over the fire until the mixture thickens, stir in the milk; when hot add the pepper and let it simmer a minute; cream the rest of the butter and beat in the lemon, onion juice and parsley; cut the eggs in quarters lengthwise, add the creamed butter to that in the saucepan, allow it to heat thoroughly, pour over the eggs and serve.

EGG TIMBALES.

For six persons use half a dozen eggs, three gills of milk, one teaspoonful of salt, one-eighth of a teaspoonful of pepper, one teaspoonful of chopped parsley, and one-fourth of a teaspoonful of onion juice, if liked. Break the eggs into a bowl and beat well with a fork, then add the seasoning and beat for a minute longer; now add the milk and stir well; butter well medium sized timbale moulds, one for each person, pour the mixture into them; put the moulds in a deep pan and pour in enough hot water to come almost to the top of the moulds. Place in a moderate oven and cook until firm in the center—for about twenty minutes—then turn out on a warm dish and pour cream or tomato sauce around them.

EGGS STUFFED WITH MUSHROOMS.

Boil half a dozen eggs hard; when done pour cold water over them, shell and cut in half lengthwise; take out the yolks, mash them and add three ounces of fresh mushrooms that have been chopped very fine and cooked tender in a teaspoonful of butter; season with salt and pepper to taste and stir in a dessertspoonful of cream, mix thoroughly. Fill the whites with this mixture, rounding the top to the shape and size of a whole yolk; sift some fine bread crumbs over the top and tiny bits of butter, brown a moment in the oven. Arrange on a dish and pour a white sauce around them in which an ounce of chopped and cooked mushrooms has been stirred, garnish with parsley and serve.

EGGS WITH CREAM.

Melt a small lump of butter in a shallow baking dish and break into it carefully six eggs, pour over them a third of a cup of boiling cream, place in a very quick oven long enough to set the whites of eggs and serve at once in the dish in which they are baked. Two or three minutes will cook them.

CURRIED EGGS.

Boil six eggs hard, cut in half lengthwise, make a white sauce and stir into it a heaping teaspoonful of curry powder; put the eggs carefully into this sauce, heat thoroughly, lift them out and place in the center of a dish. Arrange boiled rice around them, pour the sauce over the eggs, garnish with parsley and serve.

STUFFED EGGS.

Boil six eggs hard, cut in half lengthwise, take out the yolks and mash them very fine; put aside a heaping teaspoonful of it, add to the rest two teaspoonfuls of butter, three teaspoonfuls of rich cream, a few drops of onion juice, and salt and pepper to taste; mix well, fill the whites of eggs, rounding the top of each to the size of a whole egg. Make a white sauce as follows: Rub a heaping tablespoonful of butter into half a tablespoonful of flour, and stir into it a cup of boiling milk; when it is smooth and thick put the eggs into it carefully, when hot take them out, arrange daintily on a platter, pour the sauce around them, sprinkle the teaspoonful of the yolk reserved over them, garnish with parsley and serve.

FRIED STUFFED EGGS.

Prepare the eggs as in the recipe for stuffed eggs, filling the cavity of the whites evenly, and pressing the two halves together so as to make it appear as a whole egg. Take what is left of the mixture, add to it one raw egg beaten light, roll each egg in this, covering thoroughly every part of it, and fry in boiling fat. Serve around a dish of green peas, or with a cream sauce into which has been stirred, just before removing from the fire, two slightly heaping tablespoonfuls of grated Parmesan cheese.

FRICASSEED EGGS.

Put two tablespoonfuls of butter in a spider, when hot add a tablespoonful of flour, stir until smooth, then add a teaspoonful of finely minced parsley and a heaping tablespoonful of fresh mushrooms chopped very fine, and a cup of rich milk or cream. Cook until the mushrooms are tender, then add four or five hard-boiled eggs cut in quarters lengthwise; let it come to a boil and serve.

EGG CHOPS.

Take five or six hard-boiled eggs, rub the yolks through a sieve and chop the whites rather fine; put a cupful of milk in a saucepan over the fire, when hot stir into it a tablespoonful of butter rubbed smooth in two tablespoonfuls of flour with one raw egg, first adding a little of the warm milk, then pepper and salt to taste, and if liked a few drops of onion juice. Stir constantly until thick and smooth, remove from the fire, add the prepared eggs, mix well, and when cold form into the shape of chops, dip in beaten egg and fine bread crumbs and fry in boiling fat until a delicate brown; stick a sprig of parsley in the small end of each chop, arrange in the middle of a platter and serve with a white sauce around them, or green peas.

PLAIN OMELET.

Beat six eggs, the yolks to a cream, the whites to a stiff froth, add three tablespoonfuls of warm milk to the yolks and then beat into the whites of eggs. Put a small tablespoonful of butter in a spider, when it is hot turn the eggs into it, stirring gently all the time until the eggs are well set; let it brown, fold and turn out on a hot platter.

OMELET WITH CHEESE.

Follow the recipe for plain omelet; while it is cooking stir in three tablespoonfuls of grated Parmesan cheese and finish as above.

OMELET WITH MUSHROOMS.

Make an omelet as in preceding recipe. Have a quarter of a pound of fresh mushrooms chopped fine and cooked until tender in a little butter and their own juice, seasoned with salt and pepper, and add hot to the omelet just before folding it.

OMELET WITH TOMATOES.

A cup of tomatoes, the water drained from them, cooked and seasoned with pepper and salt, a teaspoonful of onion juice, and one of green pepper chopped very fine; have it hot and add to the omelet just before folding it.

POACHED EGGS WITH TOMATO CATSUP.

Poach some eggs in boiling water, trim nicely and place each egg on a round of toast buttered and moistened with a little hot milk. Have ready a white sauce, pour it over them and put on the top of each egg a teaspoonful of tomato catsup; garnish with parsley and serve.

EGGS POACHED IN CREAM.

Half a pint of cream, six eggs, salt and white pepper, and a small teaspoonful of finely minced parsley. Bring the cream to a boil in a chafing dish, break the eggs carefully, to keep the yolks whole, into the cream and cook until the whites are set—about three minutes. Have a delicate slice of toast for each egg on hot plates, lay an egg on each, pour the cream over them, sprinkle with pepper and salt and the chopped parsley and serve.

EGGS POACHED IN TOMATOES.

Put a quart can of tomatoes in a saucepan over the fire with half an onion, three cloves, a bay leaf, a sprig of parsley, a saltspoonful of sugar, and salt and pepper to taste. Cook until the onion is tender —about ten minutes—remove from the fire, press through a sieve fine enough to retain the seeds. Put this in a spider; rub an even teaspoonful of potato flour with a tablespoonful of butter, add to the sauce, and when it boils break in as many eggs as required, keep them from sticking to the pan by running a tablespoon carefully around the edges; when the eggs are set remove from the sauce, place each one on a round of nice toast and pour the sauce around them; garnish with parsley and serve.

EGGS IN A BROWN SAUCE.

Boil hard as many eggs as needed and cut either lengthwise in quarters or in round slices. Brown a tablespoonful of butter and one of flour together, add a small onion, cut fine; when thick and smooth add enough vegetable stock to make the sauce the proper consistency, season with salt and pepper and strain. Put the egg slices in the sauce, let it come to the boiling point and serve on a small platter; garnish with parsley. Half a dozen olives boiled in a little water and cut from the stones are a nice addition to the sauce.

Soups.

Bran tea, made in the proportion of a pint of bran to three quarts of water, is used by many vegetarians as a foundation for soup. Butter should be used generously with it.

A broth made from white beans is also good where a white stock is required. Pick over the beans carefully, soak over night, drain and add fresh water in the morning—three pints of water to a pint of beans—cook gently until tender. If it is to be used as a stock, strain without mashing the beans. If the water they are boiled in is hard, a small pinch of soda will soften it.

CREAM OF JERUSALEM ARTICHOKES.

Wash and peel enough artichokes to make a pint when cut in slices. Put them in a saucepan with a tablespoonful of butter, let them simmer in this for a few minutes without taking color, then cover with water and boil until tender. Rub through a sieve, put back on the stove with a quart of milk, and a tablespoonful of butter rubbed into a tablespoonful—slightly heaping—of flour, season to taste with salt and pepper, let it come to a boil. Remove from the fire and add two egg yolks, beaten with half a cup of cream, stir rapidly, and serve at once.

CREAM OF ASPARAGUS.

Prepare a bunch of asparagus in the usual way for cooking, cut off the points about an inch in length and put aside. Cover the stalks and half an onion cut in slices, with boiling water, cook until tender and press through a purée sieve with the water they were boiled in. Melt a good tablespoonful of butter in a saucepan, and stir into it half a tablespoonful of flour, add the purée of asparagus and let it come to a boil, season with salt and pepper

31

to taste. Have the asparagus points cooked tender in a little water. Have ready a pint of boiling milk, remove both from the fire and stir the milk into the soup, put the asparagus points into the tureen. Beat two egg yolks with four tablespoonfuls of cream, stir quickly into the soup and pour into the tureen.

CREAM OF LIMA BEANS.

Put over the fire a quart of lima beans in boiling water to cover them; when nearly tender add a bay leaf, half a white onion, and salt and white pepper to taste. Let them cook until very tender, remove from the fire, and mash through a colander with the water in which they were boiled. Put back in the saucepan on the range, let it come to a boil, then add a heaping tablespoonful of butter and a pint of boiling milk, stir well, remove and press through a purée sieve that it may be smooth. Beat four tablespoonfuls of cream, add when the soup is in the tureen and serve immediately. This soup is very nice when made from the best canned lima beans, using two cans and following the recipe as above.

CREAM OF CAULIFLOWER.

Cut one small cauliflower into flowerettes, reserve a tablespoonful, put the rest into a saucepan with three cups of boiling water, one small white onion, half a small celeriac cut in slices, and a bay leaf. Cook together ten minutes, drain and put the vegetables into a double boiler with two heaping tablespoonfuls of butter, a heaping tablespoonful of flour, salt and pepper to taste; steam for ten minutes. Put the flowerettes into the water the vegetables were boiled in and cook until tender, remove and put aside to keep warm, measure the water and add sufficient from the kettle to make two cupfuls, pour this over the vegetables, cook until tender and press through a fine sieve. Bring two cups of milk to the boiling point, turn the purée into this, let it boil up once, remove from the fire. Beat two egg yolks and four tablespoonfuls of rich cream together, add some of the soup to this, then mix all together, turn into the tureen, add the flowerettes and serve at once.

CREAM OF CELERY.

Take of the coarser parts of celery as much as will make two heads, wash and cut in pieces, put in a saucepan with half an onion cut in slices and cover with boiling water. Cook until tender and press through a sieve with the water in which it was boiled. Make a roux of butter and flour as in other cream soups, add the purée to it and as much boiling milk as will make it the proper consistency. Season with salt and pepper, and finish with a beaten egg yolk and two tablespoonfuls of cream, adding this after the soup has been removed from the fire.

CREAM OF CHESTNUTS.

Shell and blanch a pint of large French chestnuts. Put them in a saucepan and almost cover them with boiling water, cook until tender. Before they are quite done add a little salt. When done remove from the fire, rub through a purée sieve with the water they were boiled in. Melt a generous heaping tablespoonful of butter with an even tablespoonful of flour and add to it by degrees a pint of boiling milk, let it cook until thick, then stir in the chestnut purée and salt and pepper to taste. Let it come to a boil and serve.

CREAM OF CUCUMBERS.

Peel and cut into slices four cucumbers and one small white onion, put in a saucepan with enough boiling water to cover them, cook until tender, press through a fine sieve and pour into a saucepan, stand where it will keep hot without cooking. Have a cream sauce ready, made by melting two heaping tablespoonfuls of butter in a saucepan with two tablespoonfuls of flour, let them cook together until the mixture no longer adheres to the pan, then add gradually a quart of milk, an even teaspoonful of white pepper, a heaping teaspoonful of salt, let it boil for a few minutes until thick and pour into the cucumber purée, add two tablespoonfuls of rich cream, let it come to the boiling point, and serve at once. This is a very delicate soup, and cooking or standing on the stove after it is done will spoil it. Groult's potato flour is nicer for thickening cream soups than the common flour, but, if used, only half the quantity called for in the recipes is needed.

CREAM OF SUMMER SQUASH.

Peel the squash, slice thin, put in a saucepan and add boiling water to come nearly to the top of the squash. When nearly tender add an onion, a bay leaf and several sprigs of parsley. When tender mash through a fine sieve, return to the fire, let it come to a boil, stir in a heaping tablespoonful of butter, a heaping teaspoonful of flour, season with salt and pepper and a tiny pinch of mace. Have almost as much boiling milk as purée, remove from the fire and stir together, add two tablespoonfuls of cream, and serve at once.

CREAM OF LETTUCE.

Take two heads of nice, fresh lettuce, wash and drain and chop fine with half a small white onion, put in a saucepan with two heaping tablespoonfuls of butter, cook for about ten minutes, stirring all the time, then add two heaping tablespoonfuls of rice and a quart of milk. Let it boil for twenty minutes until the rice is perfectly tender, remove from the fire and press through a purée sieve, using a small potato masher, then strain and press again through a fine hair sieve; this will make it smooth. Season with salt to taste and a dash of cayenne pepper, and a small half teaspoonful of sugar. Put in a fresh saucepan, rub together two heaping teaspoonfuls of butter and an even teaspoonful of cornstarch and stir into the soup. Let it come to the boiling point and remove from the fire, adding at the last moment a quarter of a cupful of whipped cream. Serve with or without fried croutons.

CREAM OF MUSHROOMS.

Wash one pound of mushrooms, skin and stem them. Put the skins and stems in a saucepan with a cup of boiling water and boil ten minutes, strain and add to this water the mushroom flaps chopped very fine, and cook until tender, then press through a fine sieve. Melt two large heaping tablespoonfuls of butter in a saucepan, and stir into it two heaping tablespoonfuls of flour, and when smooth add a quart of rich milk, a whole clove of garlic, salt and pepper to taste. When it boils and thickens add the mushroom stock, let it boil up once, remove the clove of garlic, turn the soup into the tureen and serve.

CREAM OF GREEN PEAS.

Put a quart of green peas into a saucepan with a slice of white onion, cover with boiling water and cook until tender. Remove from the fire and press through a purée sieve with the water in which they were boiled. Return to the saucepan, set it back on the stove, let it come to a boil, add a pint of rich milk, salt and white pepper to taste, a dash of cayenne, and a large, generous tablespoonful of butter rubbed into an even tablespoonful of flour, adding a little of the liquid before stirring into the soup. Let it come to a boil, and add two tablespoonfuls of whipped cream just as it is poured into the tureen.

CREAM OF RICE.

Wash carefully a third of a cup of rice and put it on the fire in a pint of boiling water with a white onion and a stick of celery, let it cook slowly for an hour, then stir in a quart of milk and let it come to a boil, add a heaping tablespoonful of butter, and press through a purée sieve. Put the soup back on the fire while beating an egg yolk with two table-spoonfuls of cream and a teaspoonful of parsley minced very fine. Remove the soup from the fire, stir in the egg and cream, pour into the tureen and serve.

CREAM OF SPINACH.

Take two large handfuls of spinach, after it is washed and picked over, a small head of lettuce, a few sprigs of parsley, and a small white onion peeled and sliced. Put in a saucepan over the fire with a tablespoonful of butter, a dozen peppercorns and two cloves, and a very little boiling water, cover and stand it where the vegetables will only simmer. When they are tender rub together a generous heaping tablespoonful of butter and a heaping table-spoonful of flour, and stir it into the vegetables. Add a little boiling water, mash the vegetables smooth and press them through a fine sieve. Have the purée as thick as possible, return to the sauce-pan. Have ready a pint of boiling milk, beat two egg yolks with four tablespoonfuls of cream, pour a little of the boiling milk into them, and the rest into the purée, remove from the fire at once, then add the eggs and cream, pour into the tureen and serve immediately.

CARROT SOUP.

Take half a dozen small French carrots, wash and scrape them, put in a saucepan with boiling water and cook until tender, remove from the fire, mix with milk and press through a sieve. Melt two ounces of butter in a saucepan and rub into it a slightly heaping tablespoonful of flour, add a few grains of cayenne pepper, and stir in a little at a time the carrot purée until smooth like cream, add a few slices of cooked celery root (celeriac), and salt to taste, and pour into the purée. A tablespoonful of sherry, if liked, may be added. Serve with fried croutons.

CELERIAC SOUP.

Wash, peel and slice three celery roots, put them in a saucepan, cover with boiling water, cook until tender, and mash them through a purée sieve with the water in which they were boiled. Melt a good heaping tablespoonful of butter, stir into it a small tablespoonful of flour, and add to it the celery purée, season with a little cayenne pepper and salt to taste. Add three-quarters of a cup of macaroni previously boiled in water. As soon as it comes to a boil remove from the fire and add as much boiling milk as will make it the proper consistency. Beat two egg yolks with half a cup of cream and stir in quickly just before pouring the soup into the tureen. Care must be taken to do this off the fire, as celery soup is liable to curdle.

MOCK CLAM SOUP.

Soak a pint of marrowfat beans over night in water enough to cover them. In the morning drain, and put them on the fire with a small onion and a gallon of cold water, boil until tender and strain. Add to the stock a little summer savory, two ounces of butter and a cup of cream or rich milk, season with salt and pepper. When the soup comes to a boil, cut two slices of toast into dice, and four hard-boiled eggs in slices, put in the tureen and pour the soup over them and serve.

CORN AND TOMATO SOUP.

Grate the corn from six ears of sweet corn. Put the cobs into a quart and a pint of water and cook until all the sweetness is extracted—about half an hour. Remove the cobs and add a pint of tomatoes after they are skinned and sliced, a small onion cut in slices, a French carrot cut in dice, a quarter of a green pepper chopped fine, and the grated corn. Let it cook slowly until all are tender. Stir in two good tablespoonfuls of butter, salt and pepper to taste, pour into the tureen and serve.

SOUP CRÉCY.

Take three large carrots, wash and scrape and cut them into slices, put them in a saucepan with half an onion, a stick of celery, and a bay leaf, more than cover with boiling water and cook until tender. Remove from the fire, take out the bay leaf and rub the vegetables through a sieve with the water they were boiled in. Put back in the saucepan. Rub a generous tablespoonful of butter with half a table-spoonful of flour, and stir into the purée, add to it a cup and a half of boiling milk, stir until thick, add pepper and salt to taste. Take from the fire, and stir into it one egg yolk beaten with two tablespoon-fuls of cream. Serve at once.

CURRY SOUP.

Prepare for cooking two small white onions, two French carrots and half a turnip cut in slices, and cook slowly in a pint of boiling water until they fall to pieces, cook with them until tender a celeriac root, remove from the other vegetables and put one side. Melt two ounces of butter in a saucepan, and stir in a slightly heaping tablespoonful of flour, an even dessertspoonful of curry powder, mix well together and then add a pint of milk. Strain the vegetables through a fine sieve, but do not press them, and add the stock therefrom to the milk, etc., in the saucepan, and salt to taste. Beat half a cup of cream with two egg yolks until light, remove the soup from the fire, mix a little of it with the eggs and cream, turn it back into the saucepan, stir well together and pour at once into the tureen in which you have already placed the celeriac cut in slices. If liked, two table-spoonfuls of Madeira may be added just before the soup is turned into the tureen. Serve with croutons.

MOCK FISH SOUP.

It is better to prepare the balls for this soup first, as follows: Put in a saucepan a tablespoonful of white flour and two tablespoonfuls of Groult's potato flour, stir together and add a tablespoonful of butter and a cup of milk, mix all together and place on the stove where it is not very hot. Stir constantly until it is smooth and no longer sticks to the pan, remove from the fire, let it cool, and beat in two eggs, one at a time, season with a dash of cayenne, a few grains of powdered mace, a few drops of onion juice, a little salt and half a teaspoonful of sugar. These balls must be seasoned very delicately. Cook and drain as the spinach balls are done, using a teaspoon instead of a tablespoon. Put to one side while the soup is being made. For the soup take three French carrots, half a parsnip, half a white onion and a little green pepper chopped fine, cover with boiling water and cook until tender. Melt a generous tablespoonful of butter in a saucepan, and when it bubbles stir into it a small tablespoonful of flour, then add three cups of milk and let it come to a boil. When the vegetables are tender stir them into the thickened milk with the water they were boiled in, together with half a teaspoonful of sugar and salt and pepper to taste. Then put the balls in and let the soup come to a boil, add a teaspoonful of finely minced parsley and remove from the fire. Have one egg yolk beaten with two tablespoonfuls of cream and stir in carefully so as not to break the balls just before turning the soup into the tureen.

A NORWEGIAN SWEET SOUP.

Put a quarter of a cup of rice into three cups of boiling water with a small stick of cinnamon, and let it boil nearly an hour. About fifteen minutes before it is done add half a cup of raisins stoned. Beat two egg yolks with a heaping tablespoonful of sugar until white and creamy, then stir into them about half a cup of sweet cider, remove the soup from the fire, add a little of it to the eggs and cider, stir well, and mix all together rapidly and serve at once. Two tablespoonfuls of good sherry improves it.

ONION SOUP.

Melt two tablespoonfuls of butter in a spider, when it bubbles add four large onions, washed, skinned and cut in slices, let them simmer without browning about half an hour, then stir in a slightly heaping tablespoonful of flour. When it thickens pour in gradually a pint and a half of boiling milk, season with salt and pepper to taste, press through a purée sieve, and return to the fire. While it is getting hot, beat together two egg yolks and half a cup of cream, remove from the stove and stir the eggs and cream into it rapidly, pour at once into the tureen and serve.

SOUP OF GREEN PEAS.—No. 1.

Take from a pint of green peas two heaping tablespoonfuls and set aside. Put the rest in a saucepan with half a white onion, in boiling water. Cover tightly, letting them cook until quite tender. then mash through a purée sieve with the water in which they were boiled, and using a little more to take out all that is good of the peas through the sieve. Put back on the stove, rub a good heaping tablespoonful of butter with a small tablespoonful of flour and add to the purée of peas. Have a heaping tablespoonful of turnips and two of carrots cut into dice and cooked in as little water as possible, and the two tablespoonfuls of peas cooked until tender, add to the soup with half a teaspoonful of sugar and pepper and salt to taste. Let all this cook together while enough milk to make the soup the proper consistency is coming to a boil. Mix together, add a teaspoonful of finely minced parsley, pour into the tureen and serve.

SOUP OF GREEN PEAS.—No. 2.

Put one quart of green peas over the fire in three quarts of boiling water with three French carrots, a small turnip cut into dice and a small white onion chopped. Cover tightly and let the vegetables cook until tender. Rub two ounces of butter with a small tablespoonful of flour, add a little of the soup to this to thin it and then stir all together, add an even tablespoonful of finely minced parsley, an even teaspoonful of sugar, and salt and pepper to taste; let it come to a boil and then serve.

POTATO SOUP.

Take four large potatoes, peel and boil them tender in water, mash very fine with a small tablespoonful of butter, add as much boiling milk as will make it the right consistency. Boil in as little water as possible one tablespoonful of turnips and two of carrots cut into dice; when tender turn all into the soup, add a little cayenne and salt to taste. Just before serving beat a quarter of a cup of cream with one egg yolk, remove the soup from the fire and stir the two together as in other cream soups, and serve at once with fried croutons.

PURÉE OF VEGETABLES.

Cut fine three onions, one turnip, two French carrots and four potatoes, put in a saucepan with four tablespoonfuls of butter and a little parsley; let them cook about ten minutes, then add a tablespoonful of flour. Stir well and add two quarts of boiling milk, season with salt and pepper and a tiny bit of sugar, and when it boils take out the parsley, press the soup through a sieve and serve with croutons of fried bread.

PURÉE OF TURNIPS.

Peel and slice some young turnips, add an onion and carrot sliced, cover with boiling water and cook until tender. Mash them in the water and press through a fine sieve. To a pint of the purée have a pint of boiling milk. Return the purée to the fire, and stir into it a large heaping tablespoonful of butter and a small pinch of mace. Take the milk from the stove and stir briskly into it two egg yolks beaten with two tablespoonfuls of cream, then remove the purée from the stove and stir the eggs and milk into it, season to taste with salt and pepper and serve.

VEGETABLE SOUP.

One cup and a half of green peas, three small French carrots, and a small cauliflower cut into flowerettes, one pint of milk, half a cup of cream, a good half tablespoonful of flour, one tablespoonful of butter, and the yolks of two eggs. Wash and scrape the carrots, cut in thin slices and boil each vegetable by itself in as little water as possible. When the carrots and peas are done put them together in a saucepan with the water in which they were cooked, add the milk, put the saucepan on the fire and let it come to a boil, rub the butter and flour together, mix with a little milk and stir into the vegetables. Drain the water well from the flowerettes, and just before serving put them in the tureen. Beat the yolks of eggs and the cream together in a bowl, remove the soup from the fire, add a little of it to the eggs and cream, then turn them into the soup, stir well and pour it into the tureen.

TOMATO SOUP.

Put a generous tablespoonful of butter in a saucepan, when it is hot add half an onion chopped fine, let it stew gently for a few minutes, then add a pint of canned tomatoes, cook half an hour. Rub a heaping tablespoonful of flour and one of butter smoothly together and stir into the tomatoes. Have ready a pint of boiling milk, pour the tomatoes into a purée sieve with the boiling milk and rub through the sieve. Season with salt and pepper and a very little sugar. Return to the fire, make it hot, but be careful not to let it boil, as it will curdle. Serve at once with croutons.

BARLEY SOUP.

Put a quarter of a cup of well washed barley with a bay leaf and a small blade of mace into a pint and a half of cold water, boil slowly for three hours. Take out the bay leaf and mace and add a small onion cut fine, two French carrots cut in dice, and cook until tender, then add a pint of milk, a good heaping tablespoonful of butter, salt and pepper to taste, let it come to a boil, remove from the fire and stir into it one egg yolk beaten with two tablespoonfuls of cream.

BLACK BEAN SOUP WITH MOCK MEAT BALLS.

Soak over night a pint of black beans in a quart of water. In the morning drain, and cover with fresh water, set the saucepan on the stove; when the water comes to a boil drain it off and add a quart of fresh water. Cut fine an onion, and with a few slices of carrot and turnip and green pepper fry in a heaping tablespoonful of butter, add to the beans with a bay leaf half a dozen peppercorns, two cloves, cook until tender, press through a sieve, return to the fire, and if it is too thick add more water. Have a hard boiled egg and half a lemon cut into dice, and meat balls made from recipe given for mock meat the size of hickory nuts and boiled in water as other balls are cooked. Drop the balls into the soup, and when hot pour the soup over the lemon and egg in the tureen and serve.

Entrées.

EGG BORDER WITH RICE AND CURRY SAUCE.

Stir four eggs together, add three-quarters of a cup of rich milk, a few drops of onion juice, and salt and pepper to taste; beat a little. Have a border mould well buttered and sprinkled with finely minced parsley, pour the mixture into it, set in a pan of boiling water in the oven, cover and let it cook until firm—from five to ten minutes. Have ready some rice boiled twenty minutes in plenty of salted water and well drained, and a cream sauce into which a slightly heaping teaspoonful of curry powder has been stirred. Turn the egg border out on a hot platter, fill the center with rice, pour some of the sauce over it, and the rest around the border. Garnish with parsley and serve at once.

RICE BORDER WITH VEGETABLES OR HARD BOILED EGGS IN CREAM SAUCE.

Three-quarters of a cup of Carolina rice, picked over carefully and washed. Boil fifteen minutes in salted water. Drain off the water and have one pint and a half of boiling milk in a double boiler, stir the rice into this and cook until all the milk is absorbed, then add a tablespoonful of butter. Butter a border mould well, turn the rice into it, pressing it down so that the form will be perfect, put in the plate heater for five minutes, turn out on a platter and serve with vegetables or hard boiled eggs in a cream sauce.

A BORDER TIMBALE OF MOCK CHICKEN.

Take three-quarters of a cup of rich milk, put half of it into a saucepan with an ounce and a half of butter, let it come to a boil, and then stir into it an ounce and a half of dried and sifted bread crumbs and a good half tablespoonful of flour. Stir constantly until it no longer sticks to the pan, remove from the fire and let it cool. When cold add two heaping tablespoonfuls of finely chopped walnuts, one tablespoonful of lemon juice, one teaspoonful of onion juice, one even teaspoonful of sugar, a saltspoonful of mace, two eggs unbeaten—one at a time —and the rest of the milk, salt and pepper to taste. Beat hard. Butter well a border mould, and sprinkle with fine bread crumbs, turn the timbale mixture into it, set the mould in a pan of boiling water, cover to keep from browning, and bake from ten to fifteen minutes.

Sauce.—Put in a spider a good heaping tablespoonful of butter, let it brown, add a thick slice of onion cut in small pieces and a heaping tablespoonful of flour, stir constantly until it is a very dark rich brown, being careful not to let it burn, then add a quarter of a pound of fresh mushrooms, skinned and stemmed and cut into dice, let them cook a few minutes, then add a stock made from their stems and skins. Have a celery root that has been pared and cut into dice and cooked until tender in very little water with a bay leaf and two cloves, remove the cloves and bay leaf and turn the rest into the sauce, season with pepper and salt. Turn the timbale out on a platter, fill the center with the sauce, garnish and serve. A few truffles are a great addition. The timbale may also be served with an olive sauce.

A MOULD OF SPAGHETTINA.

Put three-quarters of a cup of spaghettina, broken in small pieces, into a quart of boiling water with an even tablespoonful of salt. Boil half an hour. Drain the water off and add a cup of milk to

the spaghettina, and cook nearly half an hour, until
the milk is almost all absorbed. Then make a cream
sauce as follows: One cup of milk in a saucepan, rub
butter the size of an egg into a slightly heaping
tablespoonful of flour, adding a little of the warm
milk, then stir into the milk on the fire, season with
salt and pepper, add two even tablespoonfuls of
grated cheese—the American Edam cheese is nice for
this—and when the sauce is thick turn the spaghettina into it, let it come to a boil, turn out on a dish,
and when cool add one egg beaten light. Butter a
border mould which holds a little more than a pint,
sprinkle it with bread crumbs, turn the mixture into
it and set the mould into a pan of hot water and
bake in a moderate oven twenty-five minutes. Have
a pint of nicely stewed tomatoes seasoned to taste
and thickened with bread crumbs and a good tablespoonful of butter. Turn the spaghettina mould out
on a platter, fill the center with the stewed tomatoes,
garnish with parsley and serve. It makes a very
pretty dish and is an excellent pièce de resistance for
dinner or luncheon.

SPINACH BORDER MOULD.

Prepare the spinach as in recipe for spinach pudding, butter a border mould, dust it with bread
crumbs, and press the spinach mixture into it, put
the mould into a pan of hot water in the oven, cover
it to prevent browning, and bake about twenty
minutes.

A FILLING FOR THE CENTER OF MOULD OF SPINACH.

Break two eggs in a bowl, add a little salt and
four tablespoonfuls of cream and beat them slightly.
Turn into a buttered tin cup and stand in a saucepan
with a little boiling water in it on the stove, cover
and cook until stiff—about three or four minutes—

remove from the fire, turn out of the mould and cut in half-inch slices and then into stars or any fancy shape preferred, or into dice. Make a cream sauce, turn the spinach mould out on a platter, put a little of the sauce in the center, then some of the egg stars, then the rest of the sauce, and finish with the egg stars.

MOCK COD FISH BALLS.

Six medium sized potatoes, washed, peeled and boiled for ten minutes in salted water. Drain and grate them while hot and stir in two heaping table-spoonfuls of butter; mix thoroughly. Season with salt, cayenne pepper to taste, and add a teaspoonful of grated onion and a saltspoonful of mace. Beat two egg yolks light and stir well into it with two heaping tablespoonfuls of cracker crumbs. Fry brown in small balls in boiling fat without crowding them in the basket, drain on kitchen paper and serve very hot on a platter, garnish with parsley.

MOCK FISH BALLS IN CURRY OR CREAM SAUCE.

Five ounces of plain boiled potatoes put through a patent vegetable strainer or mashed very fine. Add three ounces of butter and a slightly heaping table-spoonful of Groult's potato flour, two eggs slightly beaten and stirred in—a little at a time—a few drops of onion juice and salt and pepper to taste. Have a saucepan of boiling salted water over the fire, dip a tablespoon in cold water and then into the mixture and take out in oblong balls as nicely and uniformly shaped as possible, and drop them carefully into the boiling water, which must not boil too violently as the mixture is tender and would cook to pieces. Put them in without crowding and let them cook three minutes, taking them out one after another as they are done. Put in a colander to drain while preparing the curry sauce. Melt in a saucepan a heaping tablespoonful of butter and add to it a heaping teaspoonful of flour, an even teaspoonful of curry powder, stir well and add milk until of the consistency of cream sauce. Put the balls into the sauce and let it come to a boil, remove from the fire, and add a tablespoonful of good Madeira. Serve on a platter, garnish with parsley and serve. The curry powder and wine may be omitted if not liked, and the balls served in plain cream sauce.

MOCK FISH (a Norwegian dish).

Take three or four large white potatoes. Wash and peel them and boil until only half done. Grate them, and take only the part that has passed through the grater—that it may be light. Then weigh out half a pound. Beat the yolks of three eggs very light with a quarter of a cup of cream, mix with the potatoes and add three ounces of butter melted, half a teaspoonful of grated white onion, a dash of cayenne pepper, and salt to taste. Butter a mould well, sprinkle it with dried and sifted bread crumbs, put the mixture in it, and set the mould in a pan of boiling water in the oven, cover the mould and bake half an hour. Turn out carefully on a platter, pour a cream or Hollandaise sauce around it, and garnish with parsley. Serve very hot with a cucumber salad with French dressing, as a fish course.

MOCK MEAT.

Put three-quarters of a cup of milk and three ounces of butter in a saucepan on the fire. When it boils stir in three ounces of dried and rolled bread crumbs and a slightly heaping tablespoonful of flour, and half a teaspoonful of sugar. Let it cook until it no longer adheres to the pan, then remove from the fire. When it is cool, add three eggs, one at a time, beating until smooth, then add one heaping table-spoonful of chopped walnut meats, salt and pepper to taste, and a few drops of onion juice. Make into flat cakes, a little less than half an inch thick, like sausage cakes, dip them in flour, put them into a saucepan of boiling salted water and cook for three or four minutes. Take them up, drain them from the water, dip in flour again, and brown them in hot butter in a spider. Set them one side to keep hot. In another spider make a sauce. Put in a heaping table-spoonful of flour, a generous heaping tablespoonful of butter, and a heaping tablespoonful of chopped walnut meats, let them all brown nicely together, then stir in a vegetable stock that has been strained until the gravy is as thick as cream.

SPAGHETTINA CHOPS.

Spaghettina is finer than spaghetti, and for sale at Italian groceries. Half a cup of milk, half a cup of spaghettina, broken into bits, three tablespoonfuls of grated cheese, one tablespoonful of butter, half a tablespoonful of flour, and one egg. Put the spaghettina on in boiling salted water, boil for three-quarters of an hour, drain well in a colander. Make the sauce by melting the butter and stirring the flour into it until smooth, then add the cheese and milk and the spaghettina. Let it come to a boil and stir in quickly the beaten egg, let it thicken, remove at once from the fire, turn it out in a deep plate, and when cold form it into chops, dip them in beaten egg, then in bread crumbs and fry in boiling fat. They are very nice served with a tomato sauce, but good without it.

TOMATO CHOPS.

Measure three-quarters of a cup of tomatoes after the water has been drained off, put in a sauce-pan over the fire and stir into it a cupful of mashed potatoes, a heaping tablespoonful of butter, salt and pepper to taste, half a cup of grated bread crumbs. Mix thoroughly and add one egg beaten light. Remove from the fire, turn into a deep plate, let it get cold, then form in the shape of chops, dip in egg and roll in dried bread or cracker crumbs and fry a nice brown in boiling fat. Arrange on a platter and serve with tomato sauce, or place around a dish of stewed tomatoes.

SAVORY FRIED BREAD.

Cut slices of stale home-made bread about half an inch thick, shape them like chops, soak the slices in a rich, well seasoned vegetable stock until nearly saturated with it—don't allow them to become too soft—then dip in beaten egg mixed with a little milk and fry in butter in a spider until a nice brown. Serve with tomato sauce, or around a dish of stewed tomatoes.

MOCK FISH CHOPS.

Pare three good sized potatoes, cut fine and throw them into cold water to prevent them from turning dark. When all are cut drain them from the water and chop very fine—there must be two cupfuls. Have a cup of boiling milk in a saucepan and put the potatoes into it, cook until tender, but not soft, and be careful not to let them burn; when done add two generous heaping tablespoonfuls of butter, two heaping tablespoonfuls of French carrots, previously cooked in as little water as possible, and chopped very fine, one heaping teaspoonful of green pepper, one of parsley, one heaping teaspoonful of grated onion, a heaping saltspoonful of powdered mace, a dash of cayenne pepper and salt to taste. Measure two tablespoonfuls of tomatoes—after all the water has been pressed from them—chop fine and add to it one whole egg and one egg yolk beaten light, stir this into the potato mixture while on the stove, remove at once from the fire, add two heaping table-spoonfuls of cracker crumbs rolled fine, and two tablespoonfuls of fine Madeira or sherry. Turn out to cool and then form into chops, roll in egg and cracker crumbs and fry in boiling fat. Serve with cucumber salad.

FRICASSEE OF SPAGHETTINA.

Take a cupful of spaghettina, broken into small pieces, put in boiling salted water and cook for three-quarters of an hour. Drain well, have a cupful of cream sauce and stir the cooked spaghettina into it, let it come to a boil, season with salt and pepper, and add the well beaten yolk of an egg, stir well, remove at once, and turn into a hot vegetable dish and serve.

MUSHROOMS EN COQUILLE.

Wash half a pound of nice, fresh mushrooms, peel them and cut off the stems, cut the flaps into dice, and put the skins and stems in a saucepan with a cup of water, and cook for ten minutes. While these are cooking put a heaping tablespoonful of butter in a spider, when hot add the mushroom dice and let them cook until tender, then add a dessertspoonful of flour, and when it is cooked add the water the stems were boiled in, and salt and pepper to taste. If the sauce is too thick add a little more water. Stir in at the last a teaspoonful of finely minced parsley, a few drops of lemon juice and the well-beaten yolk of one egg, stir well, remove from the fire, fill the shells, sprinkle bread crumbs over the tops and a little melted butter, put in the oven for an instant to brown.

RAGOUT OF EGG PLANT.

Boil a small egg plant until tender. Peel it thinly and set aside to get cold. Cut in slices an inch thick and cover the bottom of a baking dish with them. Melt a generous tablespoonful of butter in a sauce-pan and stir into it two heaping tablespoonfuls of fresh mushrooms, a heaping teaspoonful of parsley, a heaping teaspoonful of onion, all chopped very fine, season with salt and pepper and pour over the egg plant. When it is time to put it in the oven sprinkle with Parmesan cheese and fine bread crumbs and dot with small lumps of butter, and bake until brown in a quick oven. Serve in the dish in which it is baked with the following sauce in a sauce boat.

SAUCE.—Boil the skins and stems of the mushrooms in a cup of water; while they are cooking, brown together in a spider a slightly heaping table-spoonful of butter, a slightly heaping tablespoonful of flour, and a small slice of onion cut very fine. Strain the mushroom skins and stems and add the water they were cooked in to the browned butter and flour, and when the sauce is thick and smooth turn it into a saucepan and add to it a heaping table-spoonful of mushrooms, one small cucumber pickle and two large olives, all chopped very fine. Let all simmer together for a few minutes, season to taste with salt and pepper. If the sauce is too thick add a little water. It should be like thick cream.

PATTIES OF PUFF PASTE.

Roll out some puff paste an inch thick, cut with a patty-cutter as many rounds as are needed, then with a smaller cutter stamp each round about half an inch deep. Bake in a quick oven; when done lift the centers out carefully with a knife, remove a little of the inside. When wanted heat the patty shells and fill with spaghettina in tomato sauce, mushrooms or vegetables in a cream or savory sauce, or the filling as given for spinach border mould. A few truffles cut fine are a nice addition to tomato sauce. Lay the little tops on and serve.

SAVORY RICE (a Mexican Dish).

Wash half a cup of rice, drain from the water. Put a heaping tablespoonful of butter in a spider, when hot add a small leek or white onion and the rice, fry until the rice is a golden brown—do not let it get too dark. Have ready a vegetable stock, nearly fill the spider and cook twenty minutes until the rice is perfectly dry. Every grain should stand alone. Turn out on a platter and serve with tomato sauce.

RAGOUT OF ASPARAGUS WITH MOCK MEAT BALLS.

Scrape and wash a bunch of asparagus, cut in pieces about an inch long as far as the stalks are very tender, put the remainder of the stalks with an onion into a saucepan, cover with boiling water and let it cook until tender—about half an hour. Then mash them in the water in which they were boiled through a colander. Put over the fire again, and when it comes to a boil throw in the points and cook until tender. While that is cooking make some mock meat, as given in a previous recipe, form into balls as large as a walnut. Cook them in salted boiling water for five minutes, drain them from the water, also the asparagus points from the stock, put them together in a saucepan to keep hot while making a gravy. Melt a generous heaping tablespoonful of butter in a spider, add to it when it bubbles a large heaping tablespoonful of flour, stir well until it becomes a dark, rich brown, taking care that it does not burn, add the asparagus stock, season with salt and pepper—this gravy should be like thick cream—turn it over the asparagus and meat balls, stir in a good half tablespoonful of butter, let it come to a boil and serve on a platter. Garnish with parsley.

CURRIED RICE CROQUETTES.

Put three-quarters of a cup of milk in a saucepan with butter the size of an egg, let it come to a boil, and stir into it one large cup and a half of rice that has been boiled in salted water twenty minutes. Add a slightly heaping teaspoonful of curry powder, a few drops of onion juice and salt to taste. When it comes to a boil add a beaten egg to it, stir a minute and remove from the fire. Turn it out, let it cool, and then form into cylinders and fry as usual.

MOCK FISH CROQUETTES.

Slice three medium sized potatoes, boil until tender, but not soft, chop very fine an even teaspoonful of onion with three zepherettes or small square crackers, then add the hot potatoes and chop all together, season with a dash of cayenne pepper, a saltspoonful of mace, a little salt and pepper. Make a sauce with a large heaping tablespoonful of butter, a heaping teaspoonful of flour rubbed well together in a saucepan over the fire; when smooth add three-quarters of a cup of rich hot milk, when it boils add the potato mixture, let it get thoroughly hot and stir into it a well-beaten egg, remove from the fire, turn it out to get cool. Form into cylinders, dip in egg, roll in bread crumbs, fry in boiling fat, and serve with either Hollandaise or tartar sauce.

WALNUT CROQUETTES.

Put half a pint of bread crumbs and a gill of milk in a double boiler, place over the fire and stir until thick and smooth, add a pinch of salt, three-quarters of a cup of chopped nuts and a tablespoonful of sherry. When the mixture is hot stir into it the well-beaten yolks of two eggs and remove from the fire at once. Set the mixture away to get cold, then form in any shape preferred for croquettes; dip them in egg and then in dried bread or cracker crumbs, fry in boiling fat and serve with a sauce piquante.

RAGOUT OF MUSHROOMS.

Wash half a pound of fine, fresh mushrooms, skin, stem and cut them into dice. Put the stems and skins in water to cover and stew them for twenty minutes; strain and put the mushrooms into this broth with a generous tablespoonful of butter, a teaspoonful of finely chopped onion, season with salt and pepper, cook until tender; when done add two well-beaten yolks of eggs, stir briskly and remove at once from the fire, turn out on a platter, sprinkle with a little very finely minced parsley and serve very hot.

MOCK CHICKEN CROQUETTES.

Two cups of rye bread—home-made is the best—chopped fine, one cup of chopped English walnuts. Mix together and chop again with a tablespoonful of butter, an even tablespoonful of grated onion, a scant teaspoonful of ground mace. Melt a heaping tablespoonful of butter in a saucepan with half a tablespoonful of flour and add gradually to it a cupful of rich milk; when this comes to a boil add the other ingredients, salt and pepper to taste, then stir in two well-beaten eggs, remove from the fire and add a tablespoonful of lemon juice; turn out on a platter to cool, form into cylinders, dip in egg and bread crumbs, as usual, and fry in boiling fat.

Vegetables.

Vegetables should be cooked in as little water as possible; the better way is to steam them. So much of the valuable salts are washed out by boiling in too much water.

All vegetables left over can be warmed again, either in a cream sauce, or put in a double boiler and steamed, adding a little more butter.

When pepper is used, it should always be white pepper, especially in white sauces and soups.

Never salt vegetables until they are nearly cooked; it hardens them.

The water vegetables are boiled in may be utilized in making sauces and soups; the best of the vegetables goes into it.

The water Jerusalem artichokes are boiled in becomes quite a thick jelly when cold, and makes an excellent foundation for sauces.

TO BOIL POTATOES.

Select potatoes of uniform size, wash and pare thinly, cover with boiling water and cook half an hour; when nearly done add salt. As soon as done drain from the water and set the saucepan where the potatoes can steam for a few minutes. They should be served immediately, and never allowed to remain in the water a moment after they are cooked. Potatoes are much better steamed with their skins on than boiled, as they then retain all the potashes. When they are old they should be washed, pared and covered with cold water, and allowed to stand for several hours before either boiling or frying.

POTATOES BAKED.

Select them of uniform size, wash and scrub well, cut a thin slice from each end to prevent their being soggy. They require nearly an hour to bake in a moderate oven.

TO MASH POTATOES.

Boil the potatoes carefully, drain from the water, mash fine, and to four good-sized potatoes add a heaping tablespoonful of butter, a tablespoonful or two of cream or rich milk and salt and pepper to taste. Serve at once. They must be freshly mashed and very hot to be eatable. The mashed potatoes may be squeezed through a vegetable ricer, when they are called Potatoes à la Neige.

NEW POTATOES WITH CREAM SAUCE.

Select rather small potatoes of uniform size and boil. When done drain off the water, set them back on the stove to keep hot while making a cream sauce, then put them carefully in a vegetable dish, pour the sauce over them and sprinkle with a little finely minced parsley.

BROILED POTATOES.

Take some cold boiled potatoes and cut them in rather thick slices lengthwise, dust with white pepper and salt, dip each slice in melted butter, broil over a clear fire until a nice brown. Serve with melted butter and finely minced parsley poured over them.

POTATOES À LA CRÈME AU GRATIN.

Chop cold boiled potatoes, put them in a baking dish, pour over them a cupful of white sauce nicely seasoned. sprinkle with a tablespoonful of grated Parmesan cheese or Edam cheese grated, one tablespoonful of bread crumbs, and dot all over with tiny bits of butter. Put in a quick oven for a few minutes to brown. Do not leave it in too long, or it will become dry.

STUFFED POTATOES.

Bake some medium-sized potatoes; when done cut in half lengthwise, scoop out the inside, taking care not to break the skin. Mash the potato smooth and fine with butter and a little milk, season with salt and pepper to taste, heat thoroughly, fill the skins, brush the tops over with melted butter, brown in the oven and serve.

POTATO FRICASSEE.

Put in a spider a generous tablespoonful of butter and a cup of milk, when hot add some cold potatoes cut in dice, season with pepper, salt, a few drops of onion juice. Let them get thoroughly hot, then add the beaten yolks of two eggs, stir constantly until thick. Great care must be taken not to let it cook too long, or the sauce will curdle. Pour into a vegetable dish, sprinkle a little finely minced parsley over the top and serve.

POTATOES À LA DUCHESSE.

Take cold mashed potatoes that are nicely seasoned with salt and pepper, form into little round cakes, put them on a tin, glaze over with beaten egg and brown in the oven. Arrange on a platter, garnish with parsley and serve.

SARATOGA CHIPS.

Peel some medium-sized white potatoes, and slice them very thin. It is better to have a potato slicer for these, if possible, as it cuts them so quickly and perfectly. Wash the potatoes in one or two waters, then cover with fresh water and lay a lump of ice on the top of them. Let them stand an hour, if convenient, drain in a colander, wipe dry with a towel, and fry in boiling fat—not too many at a time in the basket or they will stick together, and will not brown. Have a quick fire, and fry until brown and crisp, drain on paper, sprinkle with salt and serve.

FRENCH FRIED POTATOES.

Peel some potatoes and cut in finger lengths, not too thick, cover with ice water, and if they are old it is better to let them stand two hours. Drain, wipe dry, and fry in boiling fat as Saratoga chips—not too many at a time. When they are a nice brown lift the basket from the fat, sprinkle with salt, shake the grease from them and remove with a skimming spoon, drain on paper and serve at once.

POTATOES A LA MAITRE D'HÔTEL.

Cut cold boiled potatoes in round slices, not too thick, put in a saucepan with some melted butter, pepper and salt. When they are hot add some lemon juice and a little minced parsley and serve.

POTATOES LYONNAISE.

Fry a little onion cut in thin slices in plenty of butter; when a delicate brown add some cold boiled potatoes cut in slices of medium thickness, mixing them with the onion by tossing them together rather than stirring, as this breaks them. Cook until a nice color, drain them, put in a dish and sprinkle a little minced parsley over them.

POTATOES À LA PARISIENNE.

Peel and wash some potatoes, scoop out into little balls with a potato scoop, which is made for the purpose. Boil for five minutes, put in melted butter in a saucepan until each potato is well covered with the butter, turn them into a pan, and brown in the oven. Turn out on a dish and sprinkle with minced parsley and a little salt.

POTATOES CREAMED AND BROWNED.

Take a pint of cold boiled potatoes, cut into dice of uniform size. Have ready a pint of cream sauce, toss the potatoes in this, season with salt and white pepper to taste, put in a baking dish, sprinkle with dried bread crumbs and a tablespoonful of American Edam cheese. A few drops of onion juice, if liked, may be added before putting the potatoes into the dish. Set it in the oven a few minutes, until it becomes a golden brown and serve. Do not let it stand in the oven long or it will dry.

POTATO PUFF.

Two cupfuls of smoothly mashed boiled or baked potatoes, two tablespoonfuls of melted butter, two well-beaten whites of eggs, a cupful of sweet cream or rich milk. Stir the melted butter into the potato, then add the eggs and cream, season with salt and pepper, turn into a buttered baking dish, bake in a quick oven and serve in the dish in which it is baked.

WHITE POTATO CROQUETTES.

Boil and mash very fine four medium sized potatoes. Put half a cup of rich milk and a generous heaping tablespoonful of butter in a saucepan over the fire. When the milk comes to a boil, stir in the mashed potatoes, season with pepper and salt to taste, mix thoroughly and add the white of an egg beaten to a stiff froth, remove from the fire, turn out on a plate to cool, then make up in small cylinders, dip in beaten egg, roll in cracker crumbs and fry a delicate brown in boiling fat.

POTATO PAPA (a Mexican Dish).

Wash, pare and boil one dozen small white potatoes, mash while hot and add to them half a cup of raisins stoned and chopped very fine, twenty large Queen olives stoned and chopped fine, one tablespoonful of parsley finely minced, an even teaspoonful of sugar, and salt and pepper to taste. Mix all well together, form into an oblong shape, leaving the top rough. Brown a little butter in a spider, put the papa into it, and after a few moments' frying scatter little lumps of butter over the top and set in the oven to brown. Garnish with parsley and hard-boiled eggs cut in quarters lengthwise.

SWEET POTATOES FRIED RAW.

Peel two or three medium-sized potatoes and cut in slices about a quarter of an inch thick, fry in boiling fat—when they are a nice brown they are done—drain on paper for a moment before serving.

COOKED SWEET POTATOES FRIED.

Take several sweet potatoes cut in slices lengthwise, not too thin. Dip each slice in melted butter and then in brown sugar, and fry in a little butter.

SWEET POTATOES MASHED AND BROWNED.

Boil three sweet potatoes of medium size until done. Peel and squeeze through the patent vegetable strainer, add a heaping tablespoonful of butter, salt and pepper to taste, and enough milk to make very soft. Put in a baking dish, dot it over with tiny bits of butter and bake until brown. Serve in the dish in which it is baked. If any is left over remove the thin brown skin, make the potato into small, flat cakes and brown on both sides in a little butter in a spider.

SWEET POTATO CROQUETTES.

Three medium-sized potatoes baked and mashed very fine and beaten to a cream with one generous tablespoonful of butter, three tablespoonfuls of cream, one teaspoonful of sugar, a little salt, one teaspoonful of lemon juice, a saltspoonful of cinnamon and one egg yolk beaten very light, and add at the last the white of egg whipped to a stiff froth. Form into cones or cylinders, dip in beaten egg and bread crumbs and fry in boiling fat. Drain on kitchen paper, sift a little sugar over them and serve at once.

BRUSSELS SPROUTS.

Pick off any leaves that may be discolored and wash well a quart of Brussels sprouts, put into a saucepan with two quarts of boiling water and a saltspoonful of soda. Boil rapidly until tender— about half an hour—just before they are done add a tablespoonful of salt. Drain them in a colander, and if it is not time to serve them stand the colander over steam to keep them hot. Do not let them remain in the water. When ready to serve put the sprouts in a vegetable dish and pour over them a pint of rich cream sauce.

OKRA AND TOMATOES.

A quart of fresh or canned tomatoes—if fresh, skin in the usual way—cut them in quarters and put over the fire, let them boil until a great deal of the water has evaporated, then add a pint of fresh okra, cut in slices, cook until tender, season with a generous heaping tablespoonful of butter, and pepper and salt to taste.

BEETS.

Wash the beets carefully to avoid breaking the skin, and do not cut off the fine roots, as this will bleed and spoil them. Put on in boiling water and cook from an hour and a half to three hours. Test with a wooden skewer. Cut in slices or dice and serve with melted butter, pepper and salt. Winter beets should be soaked over night.

PURÉE OF PEAS.

When peas are old this is a very nice way to use them. Put a quart of shelled peas over the fire in sufficient boiling water to cook them. Boil until tender, drain from the water, press through a purée sieve, season with salt and pepper to taste, and a good heaping tablespoonful of butter, and if too dry a little milk or cream may be used.

PURÉE OF LIMA BEANS

may be prepared in the same way.

PURÉE OF CUCUMBERS.

Peel and slice the cucumbers and put them over the fire in as little boiling water as will cook them; when tender drain from the water, press through a purée sieve, season with salt and pepper and add a tablespoonful of butter.

STUFFED CUCUMBERS.

Peel two large, fine cucumbers, cut in half lengthwise, take out the seeds. Scrape out carefully the soft part—with a small spoon—into a saucepan. Peel and core a tart apple, chop fine with a small pickled gherkin, take from this a good tablespoonful for the sauce and put one side, then add the rest to the soft part of the cucumbers in the saucepan. Let it simmer until tender, then add butter the size of an egg, pepper and salt to taste, a few drops of onion juice, or the spoon used for stirring the mixture may be rubbed with garlic, three tablespoonfuls of grated bread crumbs, one egg beaten, stir all together, and remove at once from the fire. Put the cucumbers in a saucepan, cover with boiling water and cook gently until tender—about ten or fifteen minutes; when nearly done add a tablespoonful of salt, drain from the water, when cool enough stuff them with the dressing already prepared and press into shape, brush with egg, sprinkle bread crumbs over the top and a few tiny lumps of butter, place carefully in a pan and bake a delicate brown.

FOR THE SAUCE, take the tablespoonful of apple and pickle reserved from the stuffing, and add a teaspoonful of capers, chop all together as fine as possible, make a cream sauce and add this mixture to it on the fire and heat thoroughly. Place the cucumbers carefully on a platter and pour the sauce around them.

CUCUMBERS STUFFED WITH MUSHROOMS.

Peel two large, firm cucumbers, and cut in half lengthwise; take out the seeds. Take a quarter of a pound of fresh mushrooms, skin and stem them. Chop the mushroom flaps very fine, put them in a spider with four tablespoonfuls of melted butter and a very little water, cover and cook until tender. Remove from the fire, stir in four heaping tablespoonfuls of grated bread crumbs, salt and pepper to taste, a few drops of onion juice, and the yolk of one egg. Stuff the cucumbers with this dressing, put the halves together, fasten with wooden toothpicks or tie with string. Place in a small dish that will fit in the steamer, cover closely, and steam until tender—about three-quarters of an hour—and serve with a brown sauce made as follows:

THE SAUCE.—Put on the skins and stems of the mushrooms in boiling water. Fry a few slices each of carrot, celery top, green pepper, onion and turnip in butter, strain the water from the mushroom stems into this and stew until all are tender, strain, add a generous tablespoonful of butter and enough flour to thicken the sauce, and salt and pepper to taste. Place the cucumbers in a shallow vegetable dish, remove the strings and pour the sauce around them.

ESCALLOPED EGG PLANT.

Boil a small egg plant, cut it in half, take out the pulp, throwing away the seeds and skin, chop the pulp fine and mix with it half a teaspoonful of bread crumbs, one cup of cream or rich milk, butter the size of an egg, an even teaspoonful of finely minced parsley, pepper and salt to taste, and a few drops of onion juice. Beat all together, turn into a baking dish, cover the top with dried bread crumbs and tiny bits of butter and bake until brown. Serve in the dish in which it is baked. If any is left over, cut in slices half an inch thick and fry in butter for luncheon.

STUFFED EGG PLANT.

Take half a large egg plant, boil gently until tender, remove from the fire, take out the pulp carefully so as not to break the shell, leaving it about a quarter of an inch thick. Peel and stem a quarter of a pound of fresh mushrooms, chop very fine, reserve a heaping tablespoonful of this for the sauce, then add the pulp of the egg plant to the mushrooms in the chopping bowl, and one heaping tablespoonful of currants, washed and picked over, one even teaspoonful of grated onion, one even teaspoonful of chopped green pepper, five heaping tablespoonfuls of grated bread crumbs, four tablespoonfuls of melted butter, two tablespoonfuls of rich cream. Mix all well together, fill the shell with this mixture, press it into shape and bind carefully with string. Bake twenty minutes, remove the string and serve on a platter with the sauce poured around it.

The Sauce.—Put on the skins and stems of the mushrooms in a saucepan, cover with boiling water, cook until tender, drain, and into this water put the tablespoonful of reserved mushrooms, add salt and pepper to taste, boil a few minutes, then add a heaping teaspoonful of flour stirred into a heaping tablespoonful of butter, let all cook together until thick, and pour around the egg plant.

GREEN CORN CAKES.

One quart of grated corn, one teacup of butter melted, four tablespoonfuls of flour, two eggs, and salt and pepper to taste. Bake as griddle cakes and serve at once. These cakes are very good made of canned corn. Pound the corn in a mortar and press through a sieve.

CORN PUDDING.

Four large ears of corn grated, or a can of corn prepared as for corn cakes, one heaping tablespoonful of butter, one teaspoonful of flour, one teaspoonful of sugar, one whole egg and one yolk. Melt the butter and stir into the corn, beat the eggs and add with one pint of milk, the sugar and flour, and salt and pepper to taste. Bake in a shallow dish in a moderate oven from twenty minutes to half an hour. If it bakes too long, it becomes watery.

MOCK OYSTERS OF GREEN CORN.

A pint of grated corn, a cup of flour, one egg, two ounces of butter, three tablespoonfuls of milk, and salt and pepper to taste. Mix well and drop from a spoon in oblong cakes—to look as much like oysters as possible—into hot butter, fry brown on both sides. Serve on a platter and garnish with parsley. These may also be made of canned corn by pressing it through a colander with a potato masher to separate the hulls from it.

CORN BOILED ON THE COB.

Husk the corn and remove the silk, put in a kettle, and cover with boiling water. If the corn is young, it will cook in from five to ten minutes, as it is only necessary to set the milk. It should be served at once in a folded napkin.

CURRY OF CORN.

A can of corn, one good tart cooking apple, one tomato, a teaspoonful of finely chopped green pepper, a teaspoonful of grated onion, a teaspoonful of curry powder, a tablespoonful of chopped Brazil or English walnuts, two tablespoonfuls of butter, and salt and pepper to taste. Put the butter in a spider, when it bubbles add the apple cut in dice and onion, fry brown, then stir in the curry powder, the chopped pepper and tomato and nuts, let all simmer together for a few minutes, then add the corn, and cook gently for twenty minutes. If it is too thick a little water must be added. Serve in a shallow vegetable dish or on a platter. Fresh corn may be used. Boil and then cut from the cob, cook the cobs in the water the corn was boiled in long enough to extract all the good from them, and use this broth for the curry.

CROQUETTES OF SALSIFY AND CELERIAC.

Two roots of salsify and one large celeriac. Wash and scrape them well. Cut in pieces and cover with vinegar and water and let them stand one hour—this will prevent them from turning dark. Pour off the vinegar and water and nearly cover them with boiling water, cook until very tender, mash fine and smooth, season with pepper and salt, and a few drops of onion juice, put in a saucepan over the fire, and add a tablespoonful of butter, two tablespoonfuls of milk, and just before removing from the fire add a tablespoonful of cream and one egg, stir well, turn out into a bowl and set aside to cool. When cold make into croquettes, dip in egg and cracker crumbs and fry in a basket in boiling oil.

INDIAN CURRY OF VEGETABLES.

Equal quantities of cauliflower and potatoes, raw. The cauliflower cut into flowerettes and the potatoes into dice. Put them into a spider with a heaping table-spoonful of butter, a rounded teaspoonful of curry powder, and let them simmer for a few minutes without taking color. Then add two tablespoonfuls of tomatoes, an even teaspoonful of grated onion and one of chopped green pepper, fill up the spider with boiling water, and set it back on the stove where it will stew gently until the vegetables are tender and the water has been reduced to one-third the quantity. It should be as thick as ordinary gravy; if not, add a scant teaspoonful of flour. Just before it is done stir in a heaping tablespoonful of butter. Turn it into a shallow vegetable dish and serve very hot. The spider should be kept covered while the curry is cooking. It is very good without the green pepper. This may be warmed over, and is better the second day than the first.

KOHLRABI.

Peel them, cut in slices and pour on just enough boiling water to cook them. Cook until tender. When nearly done add salt. Make a cream sauce, season with white pepper, salt and a little grated nutmeg, if liked, toss them in this sauce, let it boil up once and serve very hot.

MARROWFAT BEANS BAKED.

Pick over carefully and wash one quart of beans, soak in water over night. In the morning drain, add fresh cold water and bring to a boil, drain again, and turn them into a four-quart stone jar, put in a generous cup of butter, two large tablespoonfuls of Porto Rico molasses, two tablespoonfuls of salt, less than a teaspoonful of pepper, and fill the jar with boiling water. Put in the oven, covering the jar with a tin cover. It must be cooked in a slow oven eight or nine hours—the water ought to last until the beans are perfectly cooked, and when done a good gravy left, about a third of the depth of the beans in the jar. Beans cooked in this way are very nutritious and easily digested. Keep them covered for two or three hours while cooking. Serve with Chili sauce.

BAYO OR MEXICAN BEANS.—No. 1.

Put one cup of Bayo or Mexican red beans to soak over night, in the morning drain off the water and put them in a saucepan with plenty of fresh water, let them cook for two hours, drain again, and add to them three fresh tomatoes, skinned and cut small, or a cup of canned tomatoes, and half an onion cut as small as the beans, then cover with boiling water and cook for one hour. Then stir in a very generous tablespoonful of butter, and salt and pepper to taste.

MEXICAN BEANS.—No. 2.

Soak over night a pint of beans and boil as in recipe No. 1 until soft. Then melt a tablespoonful of butter in a spider; when it bubbles put in a small onion chopped very fine, and fry a delicate brown. Drain the beans and turn them into the spider, add a cup of boiling water and stir until the water becomes thick like cream.

EMPARADAS (a Mexican Recipe).

Take some beans cooked as in Mexican Beans No. 1 and mash them to a paste. Then roll out some puff paste very thin—about the sixth of an inch—cut this into rounds with a large patty cutter, put a spoonful of the bean purée on the half of each round, wet the edges of the pastry, cover, press the edges together, making a half moon, brush them over with beaten egg and bake in a hot oven, or they may be fried in boiling oil or fat until a delicate brown.

FRIJOLES FRITOS.

A pint of beans cooked as in recipe for Bayo or Mexican Beans No. 1. Rub them smooth in a mortar, put them into a spider with a quarter of a cup of butter and fry for a few minutes, then add half a cup of grated Parmesan cheese, mix thoroughly and serve hot.

BROILED MUSHROOMS.

Select large flap mushrooms for broiling. Wash, skin and stem them, lay them on a dish, sprinkle with salt and pepper and pour a little olive oil over each mushroom, let them stand one hour. Broil on a gridiron over a nice clear fire. Place on a dish and serve with the following sauce: Prepare the stock as before by boiling the stems and skins in water and then straining. Mince two or three mushrooms fine, add to the stock, with a teaspoonful of minced parsley, a few drops of onion juice, a small lump of butter, cook for fifteen minutes, then add a cupful of cream, an even teaspoonful of flour wet with some of the cream and rubbed smooth. Let it all cook together for three minutes, then add the beaten yolk of an egg, stir well, remove from the fire at once and serve.

MUSHROOMS ON TOAST.

Half a pound of mushrooms, wash, stem and skin as before. Cut into dice, put in a saucepan with the juice of half a lemon, a tablespoonful of butter and a slice of onion, a sprig of parsley and one clove, tied together in a thin muslin bag. Set the saucepan on the fire and stew gently until nearly dry, then add water almost to cover them, salt and pepper to taste, and let them cook fifteen minutes. Take out the bag of onion, etc., and thicken with one egg yolk well beaten, and a small cupful of cream. Have some slices of toast on a platter, buttered and moistened with a little hot milk, pour the mushrooms over them, garnish with parsley and serve hot.

MUSHROOMS STEWED IN A CREAM SAUCE.

Make a pint of cream sauce, prepare half a pound of mushrooms as in the preceding recipe, cut into dice, and stew in the sauce until very tender. Have the toast prepared as above and pour the mushrooms over it. Garnish with parsley and serve at once. They may be served in pastry shells as an entrée, if preferred.

TOMATOES STUFFED WITH MUSHROOMS.—No. 1.

Wash, skin and stem half a pound of mushrooms, chop very fine, add two even teaspoonfuls of finely minced parsley, a few drops of lemon juice, the same of onion juice, and salt and pepper to taste. Melt two tablespoonfuls of butter in a saucepan and cook all together in this until the mushrooms are tender, then add a cupful of stale bread crumbs and one egg yolk, stir well and remove from the fire. Have half a dozen perfectly ripe tomatoes, washed and wiped, cut a slice from the top of each, take out the core and seeds, and fill with the mushroom stuffing. Bake in a moderate oven until done. The skins should be removed in the usual way before stuffing.

TOMATOES STUFFED WITH MUSHROOMS.—No. 2.

Wash and wipe the tomatoes, but do not remove the skins. Cut in half, take out the core and a few of the seeds. Fill with the same forcemeat as in the preceding recipe and cover the top with it, place in a pan with a little water to keep from burning, bake in a moderate oven until soft, remove carefully from the pan, place on a platter, garnish with parsley and serve.

ESCALLOPED TOMATOES.

Strain from a quart can of tomatoes one cupful of water. Put a layer of the tomatoes in a baking dish, season with salt, pepper and a little sugar, cover with a layer of bread crumbs, dot freely with bits of butter, then put another layer of tomatoes, and lastly a layer of bread crumbs, with bits of butter, and sprinkle with a dessertspoonful of sugar. Bake forty-five minutes, and serve in the dish in which it is baked.

TOMATOES WITH EGG.

Drain the water from a can of tomatoes, press them through a colander, put into a saucepan over the fire, season with salt and pepper, a little sugar, if acid, and a few drops of onion juice. Let them cook a little, and just before serving add the well-beaten yolks of two eggs, stir well until it thickens, and remove immediately from the fire or it will curdle.

FRENCH CARROTS IN BROWN SAUCE.

Select the smallest French carrots, wash and scrape them and boil until tender in as little water as possible. When done drain from the water, using it to make the sauce. Put a tablespoonful of butter into a spider, when hot stir in a tablespoonful of flour, stir until a dark brown, add gradually the water the carrots were boiled in, season with salt and pepper, simmer until thick and smooth, add the carrots, and when hot serve.

FRENCH CARROTS AND PEAS.

Take a pint of young peas and two bunches of French carrots, cut in slices or fancy shapes (stars or clover leaves), cook each vegetable by itself in as little water as will cook them. When they are both tender put them together into a saucepan, add a heaping tablespoonful of butter and half a tablespoonful of flour rubbed together, and if there is not enough water left, add enough to make a gravy. Canned instead of fresh peas may be used; drain the water from the peas and stew the carrots in it, and follow the recipe as above.

SPINACH PUDDING.

Make a sauce of one ounce and a half of butter, one ounce of flour, a scant half cup of rich milk, half a teaspoonful of sugar, a grating of nutmeg, if liked, and salt and pepper to taste. When this comes to a boil, add an even cupful of spinach that has been cooked and finely chopped, and from which the water has been well pressed out. Remove from the stove, and stir into it two beaten eggs. Grease a mould, sprinkle it with dried and sifted bread crumbs, turn the pudding into this, set the mould in a pan of hot water, put in the oven, cover it to prevent browning and bake nearly three-quarters of an hour. Turn out on a platter, have ready a cream sauce to pour around the pudding, garnish with hard-boiled eggs, cut in quarters lengthwise, and parsley. If any is left over, cut in slices, and warm over in a cream sauce and serve for luncheon. It will keep for days.

SPINACH BALLS.

Put a slightly heaping tablespoonful of butter, a tablespoonful of cream, and half a teaspoonful of sugar into a saucepan on the stove, mix well, and when it boils add a heaping tablespoonful of flour— as much as will stay on the spoon—let it come to a boil, and then add three-quarters of a cup of cooked and finely chopped spinach, beat well and remove from the fire. When cold add two eggs, one at a time, season with salt and pepper to taste and half a saltspoonful of powdered mace. Have a saucepan of boiling water, slightly salted, on the stove; dip a tablespoon in cold water, and then take up enough of the spinach mixture to make an oblong cake, in shape like an egg cut in half lengthwise, then dip the spoon in the boiling water and let the cake float off. Use all the mixture in this way. The balls will cook in four or five minutes, and they must not boil too fast or they will break. Let them drain in a colander while making a cream sauce, and when the sauce is made put the balls into it and let them come to a boil, turn out on a platter and garnish with parsley.

TOMATOES AND MUSHROOMS.

Put on a pint of tomatoes in a saucepan and cook for fifteen or twenty minutes until nearly all the water has evaporated, season with salt and pepper, add a generous tablespoonful of butter, a table-spoonful of bread crumbs and half a pint of fresh mushrooms chopped fine. Cook until the mushrooms are tender. Have some bread cut in nice slices toasted and slightly moistened with warm milk. Pour the tomatoes and mushrooms over it and serve very hot.

TO BOIL RICE PLAIN.

Wash half a cupful of rice, drain from the water, have on the fire a very large saucepan nearly full of salted boiling water. Turn the rice into this and boil hard for twenty minutes, pour all into a colander, drain well, and put the rice in a smaller saucepan on the back of the stove, where it will be kept warm, without cooking, until all the moisture has evaporated. Then serve.

CAULIFLOWER WITH DRAWN BUTTER.

Select a nice white cauliflower, take off all the leaves, and cut enough of the stem off to allow it to stand well in the dish it is to be served in. Put it into a saucepan, cover with boiling water, and when it is nearly done add salt, as cooking it long with salt turns it brown. The usual time to cook a cauliflower is about twenty minutes. Try it with a fork, and if it is tender remove carefully from the water, let it drain in a colander while preparing a drawn butter. Then put into a hot vegetable dish, pour the sauce over and serve.

FOR THE DRAWN BUTTER.—Melt a large heaping tablespoonful of butter, and stir into it a heaping teaspoonful of flour, let them cook together without browning and add by degrees a cup of hot milk.

ESCALLOPED CAULIFLOWER.

Cut a cauliflower into flowerettes, cover with boiling water into a saucepan and cook until tender, let them drain in a colander while the sauce is being prepared. Make the usual cream sauce, enough to cover the cauliflower. When the sauce is done add two heaping tablespoonfuls of American Edam or grated Parmesan cheese, put the flowerettes into a baking dish, pour the sauce over them, sprinkle the top with a little of the cheese, and stand the dish in the oven for a few minutes to brown.

ESCALLOPED SPAGHETTINA.

Put a good half cupful of spaghettina, broken in bits, into a saucepan of boiling water with an even tablespoonful of salt, boil three-quarters of an hour, turn into a colander and let it drain while the sauce is being made. Prepare it exactly as for escalloped cauliflower and finish in the same way.

CHESTNUT PURÉE.

Shell some large imported chestnuts and put over the fire in boiling water, let them cook for a few minutes, rub the skins off, and cover again with fresh boiling water, boil until tender. Press through a sieve, and season with butter, pepper and salt.

PUREE OF DRIED WHITE BEANS.

Pick over and wash a pint of beans and soak over night. In the morning drain off the water, put the beans into a saucepan with cold water to cover them, and cook until tender—a little more than an hour. Press through a sieve, add a generous tablespoonful of butter, salt and pepper to taste, put into a saucepan, make very hot and serve.

SQUASH PUDDING.

A large heaping cup of Hubbard squash, measured after it is baked and mashed smooth, a generous heaping tablespoonful of butter, melted and stirred into the squash, a heaping teaspoonful of flour mixed with four tablespoonfuls of milk and one egg beaten light, salt and pepper to taste. Mix well and turn into a buttered pudding dish and bake about twenty minutes. Serve in the dish in which it is baked. If any is left over, make it up into little round cakes and brown in butter for luncheon.

SQUASH FRITTERS.

A heaping cupful of Hubbard squash baked and mashed, stir into it a heaping tablespoonful of butter, a heaping tablespoonful of flour, a cup of milk, salt and pepper to taste, and one egg beaten light. Mix well and bake or fry as griddle cakes.

SUMMER SQUASH.

Wash and peel two large summer squash, cut in small pieces and remove the seeds, cover with boiling water and cook until tender. Drain in a colander and press gently as much of the water out as possible with a potato masher, then mash through the colander into a saucepan, put it on the stove and let it cook until the squash is quite dry, taking care that it does not burn. Then add four heaping tablespoonfuls of butter, a teaspoonful of sugar, and salt and pepper to taste.

RICE CROQUETTES.

Put three-quarters of a cup of milk in a saucepan over the fire, with a generous tablespoonful of butter, a heaping teaspoonful of sugar, and when it comes to a boil add a cup and a half of boiled rice, a salt-spoonful of powdered cinnamon or nutmeg, if preferred, and salt to taste. Mix well, let it come to a boil and add a beaten egg, remove from the fire, turn into a plate to get cold, form into cylinders and cook in boiling fat.

FRICASSEE OF CELERIAC.

Wash and peel the celery roots, cut them into dice and cook until tender in as little water as possible, and when nearly done add a little salt. Make a sauce of two tablespoonfuls of butter and one tablespoonful of flour cooked together until smooth without browning. Then add a cup of rich milk, and when this boils turn the celery dice with the water in which they were boiled into the sauce, season to taste with salt and pepper. When ready to serve beat one egg yolk with a tablespoonful of cream and stir carefully into it, remove at once from the fire, pour into a vegetable dish, sprinkle with a little parsley minced fine, and serve.

YELLOW TURNIP RAGOUT.

Take one large yellow turnip, peel, wash and wipe dry, cut in oblong pieces. Brown a good lump of butter in a spider, simmer the turnip slices in this until nicely browned, taking care not to burn them. Put all into a saucepan with only water enough to cook them tender, cover tightly, when done, brown a little butter and flour together to make the gravy the proper consistency, season with pepper and salt and serve.

TOMATOES STUFFED WITH CHEESE.

Cut six tomatoes in half, scoop out part of the inside and put this in a saucepan and cook until nearly all the water has been absorbed, then add half a teaspoonful of sugar, one heaping tablespoonful of butter, two heaping tablespoonfuls of grated cheese, two heaping tablespoonfuls of dried bread crumbs, pepper and salt to taste, and a few drops of onion juice. Sprinkle the tomatoes with salt, pepper, a little sugar and grated cheese, then fill them with the dressing, dot them with tiny bits of butter and sift over them a few bread crumbs. Melt half a teaspoonful of butter in a baking pan, put the tomatoes in and bake twenty or twenty-five minutes. Take them out carefully when done, arrange on a dish, make a little gravy in the pan in which they were baked by adding a little more butter, half a cupful of milk, a heaping teaspoonful of flour, and salt and pepper to taste. Serve in a sauceboat.

JERUSALEM ARTICHOKES.

Wash and peel a dozen artichokes, selecting them as nearly the same size as possible. Cover with boiling water and cook until tender, drain at once and pour over them a cream sauce, sprinkle a little finely chopped parsley over them and serve.

ASPARAGUS.

Scrape and wash as much asparagus as is needed, cut the stalks the same length, tie in bunches and put over the fire in boiling water, and when nearly done add a little salt. Boil until perfectly tender, drain, put in a dish, remove the strings and serve very hot with sauce Hollandaise or a simple cream sauce.

POINTES D'ASPERGES.

Cut off the tender green tips of asparagus about an inch and a half long, cover with boiling water and cook until tender. Add salt just before they are done. Drain and put the points into a saucepan with butter, salt and pepper and a few spoonfuls of cream or Hollandaise sauce, mix well and do not let it cook after the sauce is added. A little nutmeg may be used if liked. Serve very hot.

PURPLE CABBAGE WITH CHESTNUTS.

Shred fine as for cold slaw half a purple cabbage, put half of this into a saucepan, dot with a tablespoonful of butter, sprinkle over it a heaping tablespoonful of sugar, a slightly heaping tablespoonful of flour, a little salt and pepper, then the rest of the cabbage with the same quantity of butter, sugar, etc., as before, and pour over all a quarter of a cup of vinegar and a cupful of cold water. Cover tightly, let it cook slowly until done, put it where it will only simmer for two hours. If not sour enough add more vinegar. Be careful that it does not burn. Serve in a vegetable dish and garnish with large Italian chestnuts that have been boiled and blanched.

PARSNIP CROQUETTES WITH WALNUTS.

Take two good-sized parsnips, peel and cook them until tender in as little water as possible. When done press the water carefully from them and mash them smooth and fine through a colander, put them back into the saucepan over the fire again, and add to them two heaping tablespoonfuls of chopped walnut meats, a good heaping tablespoonful of butter and a tablespoonful of rich cream, stir well together and add at the last one egg well beaten. Remove from the fire and turn out on a plate to cool, then form into cylinders, dip in egg and bread crumbs and fry in boiling fat.

PARSNIPS FRIED.

Boil them until tender, cut them in slices length-wise and fry brown in a little butter.

PARSNIP FRITTERS.

Wash and scrape them and cut in slices, cover them with boiling water, cook until tender, mash them through a colander, return them to the fire, add to two large parsnips, a tablespoonful of butter, salt and pepper to taste, and one egg beaten well. Mix thoroughly, remove from the fire, and when cool make into small flat cakes and fry in a little butter. Serve hot.

TO COOK STRING BEANS.

String thoroughly, cut in half, then in half length-wise, throw into boiling water and let them come to a boil. Remove from the fire, drain, cover with cold water and let them stand in this until it is time to cook them, then drain again, cover with boiling water and cook for fifteen minutes, and when almost done add salt. When tender, drain, add a lump of butter, and salt and pepper to taste.

SPANISH ONIONS STUFFED.

Take two large Spanish onions, wash and skin and tie them to prevent breaking. Put them into a saucepan over the fire, cover with boiling water, cook until they can be pierced with a broom straw— from two to three hours, according to size. When done, drain and carefully take out the centers, leaving about a quarter of an inch for the shell. Have ready a stuffing made from a quarter of a pound of mushrooms prepared as before. Put these and the centers of the onions into a chopping bowl and chop very fine. Cook them together until the moisture from the onions has almost evaporated, then add a generous heaping tablespoonful of butter, a tablespoonful of rich cream, and three heaping tablespoonfuls of grated bread crumbs, salt and pepper to taste. Fill the onion shells with this mixture, smooth the tops nicely, sprinkle with bread crumbs, brush with egg and a little butter. Put in the oven and brown about ten minutes, and serve with the following sauce: Rub a generous heaping tablespoonful of butter and a heaping tablespoonful of flour together. Put a small teacup of milk into a saucepan on the fire, when hot stir in the butter and flour and a quarter of a pound of mushrooms prepared as before and chopped very fine, season with salt and pepper to taste. Place the onions on a platter and pour the sauce around them, garnish with parsley and serve.

STUFFED CELERIAC WITH SPANISH SAUCE.

Put over the fire in a saucepan three-quarters of a cup of rich milk and three ounces of butter, let them come to a boil, then add three ounces of dried and sifted bread crumbs and an even tablespoonful of flour. Let it cook, stirring all the time until it is a smooth paste and detaches itself from the sides of the pan, remove from the fire and set it aside to cool. When cold beat three eggs light, stir in a little at a time, beating well until the mixture is smooth and all the beaten egg used, then add a heaping teaspoonful of sugar, three heaping tablespoonfuls of walnut meats chopped fine, two tablespoonfuls of rich cream, and salt and pepper to taste. Take four large, fine celeriac roots, clean, scrub and scrape them. Cut off a slice from the top of each to make a cover, then with an apple corer remove the inside, taking care not to pierce the root, leave a shell a quarter of an inch thick. Fill each with the dressing, leaving fully half an inch at the top for it to swell. Place the cover on each, tie well the roots to prevent breaking in the cooking, stand them in a saucepan with water to reach not quite to the top of the roots, and put in all the celeriac removed from the roots, boil gently until tender—about an hour—adding boiling water from time to time as it evaporates. When they are tender take them out of the water and put them aside, keeping them hot. Strain the water they were boiled in, form what is left from the stuffing into small cylinders, boil five minutes in the strained stock, take them out and put with the roots to keep warm. Then take a generous tablespoonful of butter, an even tablespoonful of flour, brown them together in a spider, add two heaping tablespoonfuls of chopped walnuts and let them brown a little, then stir in gradually the stock the roots were boiled in and cook until it thickens. Arrange the roots in the center of the platter, the cylinders around them and pour the sauce over all. Garnish with parsley, putting a tiny sprig of celery leaves in the top of each root.

SPRING CABBAGE STEWED.

Cut the cabbage very small, throw into a saucepan, cover with boiling water, when nearly done add salt. Cook until tender, drain well in a colander. Make a rich cream sauce—it must be quite thick, as the cabbage will thin it—add a saltspoonful of mace, then the cabbage, let it come to a boil and serve.

SPRING CABBAGE WITH CREAM SAUCE.

Boil a young cabbage or part of one until perfectly tender, when done drain all the water from it in a colander, place in a vegetable dish and pour over it a rich cream sauce.

SPRING TURNIPS IN CREAM SAUCE.

Pare and cut into dice some young turnips, cook them tender in as little water as possible, salt when nearly done. Have ready a cream sauce, nicely seasoned, and after draining the turnips put them into the sauce, let them come to the boiling point and remove immediately from the fire, turn them into the serving dish, sprinkle a little finely chopped parsley over the top and serve. A tiny grain of mace added to the sauce is an improvement, but it must be used with great care.

WHITE BREAD BALLS.

Take four ounces of bread from which the crust has been removed, cut it into dice. Put half a cup of milk in a saucepan with two ounces of butter and a teaspoonful of sugar, let it come to a boil, then stir in the bread and continue stirring until it no longer cleaves to the pan, remove from the fire. When cool stir into it two eggs, one at a time, and a little salt. Cook in boiling water, as described for other balls, and serve in a cream sauce as a vegetable. (See spinach balls, page 74.)

NOODLES.

Beat the yolks of two eggs with a little salt and one tablespoonful of cold water and stir in enough flour to make a very stiff dough. Roll out as thin as paper and then roll it up; let it stand for an hour, and then cut fine with a sharp knife. These will keep any length of time, and can be used in soups, as a vegetable or in a pudding.

NOODLES À LA FERRARI.

Prepare the noodles as above, and cook in boiling salted water from twenty to twenty-five minutes. Drain well. Have ready a tomato sauce, stir the noodles into it, turn into a baking dish, sprinkle well with grated Parmesan cheese and brown in a quick oven.

GNOCCHI À LA ROMAINE.

Put two ounces of butter in a saucepan over the fire with two tablespoonfuls of milk. When this comes to a boil stir in four ounces of flour; then add a cup of milk, let it cook, stirring all the time until it no longer adheres to the pan, remove from the fire, let it cool and then beat in three eggs, one at a time, two heaping tablespoonfuls of grated Parmesan cheese, a saltspoonful of mace and a dash of salt. Set it away to get cold, make it into small balls. Have a large saucepan of boiling, salted water on the stove, drop the balls into it and let them boil five minutes, take them out with a skimmer and drain well. Have ready a cream sauce, put the balls in this, and when they are hot turn into a baking dish, sprinkle with Parmesan cheese and bake until brown in a quick oven.

Salads.

MAYONNAISE DRESSING.

One-half teaspoonful of mustard, one-half tea-spoonful of sugar, one teaspoonful of salt and a dash of cayenne pepper; then add two raw egg yolks, beat well and stir in a teaspoonful of strong vinegar; add very carefully, drop by drop, a scant three-quarters of a cup of best olive oil, and as it thickens half a teaspoonful of vinegar. This recipe never fails, if the directions are carefully followed. The eggs and oil should be kept in the refrigerator and be ice cold. Lemon juice may be used, instead of vinegar, if preferred.

CREAM SALAD DRESSING.

One-quarter of a cup of strong cider vinegar, one cup and a quarter of water, one-half cup of butter, one teaspoonful of mustard, one teaspoonful of salt, one tablespoonful, slightly heaping, of corn starch, one teaspoonful of sugar, a dash of cayenne pepper and the yolks of four eggs. Put the vinegar and water in a saucepan and when it boils add the butter. Beat the yolks of eggs and the other ingredients together with an egg-beater, making it quite foamy and light; pour the boiling vinegar and water upon this mixture, which will partially thicken. The bowl in which it is mixed should be placed in a pan of hot water on the stove, beating it all the time with the egg-beater. Just before it reaches the boiling point remove and turn it out into a cold bowl, beating hard for a few minutes. When perfectly cold pour it into a glass jar, fasten down the top and keep in refrigerator.

FRENCH DRESSING.

One tablespoonful of vinegar, three tablespoonfuls of olive oil, a saltspoonful of salt and one of white pepper, and a few drops of any good sauce. Lettuce should be well washed in very cold water, leaf by leaf, and drained in a basket, which comes for the purpose, then placed on the ice, and at serving time put into the salad bowl. Lettuce should never be cut with a knife, but torn with a fork and spoon, and it should not be allowed to stand after the dressing is poured over it.

TOMATO ICE SALAD.

Put a quart can of tomatoes in a saucepan over the fire with half an onion, a slice of green pepper, if convenient, three cloves, two bay leaves, a sprig of parsley, a teaspoonful of sugar, and pepper and salt to taste. Cook until the onion is tender—about ten minutes—remove from the fire, press through a sieve fine enough to retain the seeds. When cold freeze as water-ice and mould—a melon mould is very pretty for it—pack in salt and ice in the usual way; turn it out in a nest of crisp young lettuce and serve with a mayonnaise dressing in a sauceboat.

* TOMATO JELLY.

One can of tomatoes put on to heat in a granite or porcelain-lined saucepan with a large slice of onion, one clove, two bay leaves, a teaspoonful of chopped green pepper, salt to taste and a little sugar. Soak half a box of gelatine in a little water for half an

---

* We have as yet in this country no substitute for animal gelatine. I have experimented with carrageen or Irish moss and the Sea-moss Farine preparation, and find them unsatisfactory. It is impossible to make a clear jelly with them, and by soaking in water to destroy the sea flavor, the solidifying property is lost. In England they have a vegetable gelatine (Agar Agar) which makes, I am told, a clear, sparkling jelly, and is said not to be expensive. I trust that before many months it may be obtainable here. I have ventured, therefore, to give a few recipes where gelatine is used, knowing that there will be something to replace it. Groult's tapioca and potato flour are said to be unadulterated, and with fresh fruit juices make nice and wholesome desserts, especially for children. These preparations are made in France, and put up in half-pound packages, and sold by all of our leading grocers.

hour, and after the tomatoes have simmered fifteen minutes let them come to a boil and pour over the gelatine to dissolve it; strain through a very fine sieve into a bowl, let it get perfectly cold, and when it begins to thicken stir well and turn into an earthenware mould. It looks prettier in a round one. Set on ice. Serve the jelly on a round dish in a bed of fresh, crisp young lettuce leaves, and place a spoonful of tender, finely-cut celery in each leaf, and pour mayonnaise around it. The jelly is better made the day before it is needed.

SPAGHETTINA AND CELERY SALAD.

Take some cold boiled spaghettina, chop—not too fine—and cover with a French dressing, and let it stand on the ice until serving time. Have an equal quantity of fresh, crisp celery cut fine, mix with the spaghettina, cover with a mayonnaise dressing and garnish with tender lettuce leaves.

SALAD OF FAIRY RINGS AND PUFF BALL MUSHROOMS.

Have both very fresh; cook the fairy rings until tender, set aside to get cold, then put on the ice. Take an equal quantity of puff ball raw, chop fine, mix with the rings, turn into a nest of tender young lettuce, cover with a mayonnaise dressing and serve.

SALAD OF FRESH FRUIT.

Peel and cut into dice enough fruit, peaches, tart plums, orange and banana to fill a cup and a cupful of crisp celery cut fine; have both ice cold; at serving time mix and cover with a cream dressing and garnish with celery tops.

*CUCUMBER JELLY.

Half a box of gelatine soaked for an hour in half a cup of cold water. Remove the seeds from a small

*This jelly may be colored a delicate green by using extract of spinach (see recipe, page 164). Its appearance is much improved thereby.

green pepper, peel and cut into slices two large, fine, fresh cucumbers, or three small ones and a small white onion. Put in a saucepan, add a bay leaf and a bouquet of parsley, cover with boiling water and cook until tender; remove the parsley and bay leaf, add a saltspoonful of sugar, salt to taste—more than a teaspoonful will be required—and press through a fine sieve. There should be, when strained, two cups and a half. Pour it over the soaked gelatine—if it is not hot enough to dissolve the gelatine place the saucepan over the fire for a moment—then run it through the same sieve again; set aside in a bowl to cool. When perfectly cold and beginning to congeal, stir it well and pour into a pretty, round mould; set it on ice until ready to serve. Turn it out on a plate and arrange fresh, crisp, young lettuce leaves around it, into each of which put a spoonful of mayonnaise or cream dressing.

WALNUT AND CELERY SALAD.

Three cupfuls of fresh, crisp celery cut fine and two cupfuls of walnuts, carefully shelled that they may be as little broken as possible. Put the walnuts in a saucepan with a small onion sliced, a bay leaf, a clove and twelve pepper corns, cover with boiling water, let them cook for ten or fifteen minutes, remove from the fire, drain and throw the nuts into cold water, remove the skins and let them get cold; then set on the ice until it is time to serve. Mix them with the celery, add mayonnaise or cream dressing, put on a dish or in a salad bowl, garnish with the tender green celery leaves and serve.

PINEAPPLE AND CELERY SALAD.

Equal parts of celery and shredded pineapple. Have the celery of the very tenderest, using only the best of the heads. Select a perfectly ripe, fresh pineapple, pare it, removing the eyes carefully, and shred the fruit with a silver fork and cut into small pieces with a silver fruit knife; put the celery, cut fine, and the shredded pineapple, each by itself on the ice, that they may be very cold. When it is time to serve the salad, mix them together, put on the salad dish, cover with mayonnaise dressing, garnish with the green celery leaves and serve at once.

FRUIT SALAD.

Equal quantities of grape fruit or oranges, bananas, apples and celery. Peel the grape fruit or oranges, carefully removing all the bitter white skin, cut the pulp, the bananas and apples into small dice and the celery fine as for other salads; put the orange and apple together; the latter will absorb the juice of the orange. Set all on ice;—these fruit salads must be ice cold. When it is time to serve, mix the fruit and celery together, put into a salad bowl, cover with the cream dressing into which has been stirred a third as much whipped cream as there is dressing, and add a little more salt to it in mixing. Serve in a bed of tender lettuce leaves.

POTATO SALAD.

Prepare equal parts of cold boiled potatoes and fresh, crisp celery, cut in small pieces which will look attractive when mixed with the dressing; cut in dice four cold, hard boiled eggs, and mix them in lightly with the potato and celery when adding the dressing. Use mayonnaise or cream dressing with this salad, garnish with dainty celery tops and serve.

SALAD OF TOMATOES STUFFED WITH CELERY.

Select nice, smooth, firm tomatoes, one for each person; blanch them in the usual way, cut a slice from the stem end and remove the core and some of the seeds; set on the ice to get cold. Prepare some celery, shredding it fine and using only the very tender part;

mix it with mayonnaise dressing, stuff the tomatoes, allowing the celery to come above the top, serve each in a leaf or two of crisp lettuce and pour some mayonnaise around them. Salads should be ice cold.

CELERIAC AND LETTUCE SALAD.

Boil two or three celery roots in water with a little salt until tender; drain and let them get cold. Cut them in thin slices, make a nest of crisp lettuce and put the celery slices in the center. Serve with a French dressing.

RAW JERUSALEM ARTICHOKES AND LETTUCE SALAD.

Wash and peel the artichokes, cut in very thin slices and put into an earthen bowl with vinegar and water with a lump of ice in it. The vinegar will prevent them from turning dark. When ready to serve, place in the center of nice, fresh lettuce and serve with a French dressing.

SALAD À LA MACÉDOINE.

Take several kinds of cold boiled vegetables in equal quantities, such as green peas, string beans, flowerettes of cauliflower, asparagus points, a small potato and a French carrot cut in small dice, and a little green pepper if liked; mix together and serve in a nest of fresh, crisp lettuce with a French dressing, or mayonnaise, if preferred.

ASPARAGUS SALAD.

Select very tender asparagus, cut off all the woody part and boil until tender, set aside to get cold, and then put on ice until serving time; arrange nicely on a platter or individual plates and serve with either mayonnaise or French dressing.

CUCUMBER SALAD.

Peel and cut in very thin slices, lay in a bowl, cover with water, sprinkle a little salt over them and put a lump of ice on top, let them remain until serving time, drain off the water and serve in a glass dish with a French dressing. They should be very cold and crisp. A little green pepper, chopped very fine, is an addition; also to rub the spoon used in mixing with a clove of garlic gives a piquancy to the salad.

COLD SLAW.

Select a firm cabbage and shave very fine on a cutter that comes for this purpose. Use the cream dressing or French dressing with a little dry mustard added.

TOMATO SALAD.

The tomatoes should be blanched in the usual way, and either sliced or cut in dice or served whole; or they may be cut in quarters, not quite separating them, and arranged in a bed of lettuce with a spoonful of mayonnaise on top of each tomato and the lettuce garnished with the same.

ENDIVE

is excellent with French dressing.

EGG SALAD.

Boil three eggs hard, cut in half lengthwise, remove the yolks and mash fine. Mix together in a saucepan the third of a teaspoonful each of dry mustard, salt and white pepper, a saltspoonful of curry powder, a few drops of onion juice, a teaspoonful of vinegar, two tablespoonfuls of egg well beaten, two teaspoonfuls of olive oil and a tablespoonful of rich cream. Put the ingredients together in the order in which they are named, beat well, set the bowl over the steam of the kettle and stir constantly until thick and creamy; remove and stir in the mashed egg yolks, a little at a time, and set on the ice to get very cold. To serve, fill the whites of egg, dividing the mixture among them, put each half egg on two or three leaves of tender lettuce, with mayonnaise dressing around them.

Desserts.

APPLE BETTY.

Two cups of tart cooking apples, chopped, a cup and a half of stale bread crumbs—bakers' bread is the best; four heaping tablespoonfuls of sugar, one generous tablespoonful of butter, and the grated rind of one lemon. Butter a pudding dish, divide the ingredients into four layers, beginning with apples and finishing with bread crumbs. Sprinkle the sugar and lemon over the apples and cut the butter into tiny lumps and scatter over the crumbs. Bake three-quarters of an hour in a moderate oven. Serve with cream or hard sauce.

APPLE CHARLOTTE.

Pare, core and quarter eight or nine good cooking apples, put them into a double boiler with two tablespoonfuls of butter, half a cup of sugar, the juice and grated rind of a lemon; cook until tender. Take a plain mould that holds three pints, butter it well, line the bottom and sides with very thin slices of home-made bread. Remove the crust, dip each slice in melted butter, fit them evenly together in the mould, fill with the apples, cover with the bread, dredge it with sugar and bake three-quarters of an hour in a quick oven. Have a hot platter, lay it over the top of the charlotte, turn it over, and lift off the mould. Serve hot with or without sauce or cream.

APPLE CROQUETTES.

Peel, core and quarter four good-sized cooking apples, cut in thin slices and put them in a granite ware saucepan over the fire with a small tablespoonful of butter, a heaping tablespoonful of sugar, the grated rind of half a lemon and a saltspoonful of cinnamon: cover tightly and cook until tender, taking care that it does not burn. When done add an even tablespoonful of Groult's potato flour, mixed with a very little water, then stir in one beaten egg, and remove from the fire. Turn into a deep plate to get cold, form in cylinders, dip in egg and dried bread crumbs and fry in boiling fat. Sift powdered sugar over them and serve hot, with or without cream.

APPLES STEWED WHOLE.

Take some nice, tart cooking apples, pare and put them into a saucepan with the juice of two lemons and the rind of one; cover with water, cook slowly until they can be pierced with a straw, take them from the water with a draining spoon. Make a syrup, allowing half a pound of sugar to a pound of fruit, use as much of the water the apples were cooked in as will dissolve the sugar; when it comes to a boil add the apples and cook until clear. Take the apples out, core them and fill with a fruit jelly, if liked, boil down the syrup and pour over the fruit. Serve very cold with whipped or plain cream. Bartlett pears may be cooked in the same manner, serving them whole.

APPLE SOUFFLÉ.

Seven tart, juicy apples, pared and cored, and cut fine. Put them over the fire in a double boiler without any water, steam until tender, then stir into them two tablespoonfuls of butter and one cup of sugar, remove from the fire, and turn it into a bowl to cool. When it is cold beat in the yolks of four eggs, whipped very light, a little grated lemon peel, and then add alternately the whites of the eggs, beaten to a stiff froth, and a cup of stale bread crumbs. Beat hard for a few moments and turn into a buttered pudding dish and bake in a moderate oven about one hour. Cover it while baking until ten or fifteen minutes before it is done, so that it will not form a hard crust and become dry. Serve warm in the dish in which it is baked.

APPLE CUSTARD.—No. 1.

Grate some good, tart cooking apples—enough to measure one quart. Beat a generous tablespoonful of butter and seven tablespoonfuls of sugar to a cream, add to this four egg yolks beaten light, then the apples and the grated rind of a lemon, and lastly the whites of four eggs beaten to a stiff froth. It can be baked in puff paste or without. Serve cold.

APPLE CUSTARD.—No. 2.

Pare, core and quarter half a dozen fine, large cooking apples, put them in a double boiler with the grated rind of half a large lemon, cook until tender, and press through a sieve; there must be three-quarters of a pint of the purée. Add an ounce and a half of granulated sugar and set it away to get cold. Then beat three eggs very light and stir gradually into a pint of rich milk alternately with the apple purée, add a little cinnamon, pour it into a pudding dish and bake about twenty minutes. Serve cold with a little cinnamon and sugar sifted over it.

BAKED APPLE DUMPLINGS.

Sift a pint of flour with a teaspoonful of baking powder and half a teaspoonful of salt. Put a quarter of a pint of butter into it and chop it fine with a knife; mix it well—do not use the hands; then add milk enough to moisten it, about a quarter of a pint. Dust a pastry board with flour, take the dough from the bowl, roll lightly into a sheet about an eighth of an inch thick, cut into squares large enough to hold an apple. Pare and core medium sized cooking apples, fill with sugar and a little cinnamon, put in the middle of the square and draw the corners up over the apples, moistening them with a little white of egg or water to make them stick. Brush over the dumplings with beaten egg and bake in a good oven. The time will depend upon the apples—about half an hour. Serve with cream.

APPLE FLOAT.

Have a pint of apple purée, made from nice tart apples, sweetened to taste and flavored with the grated rind of lemon and cinnamon, or nutmeg if preferred. Set it on the ice that it may be very cold, beat the whites of two eggs to a stiff froth and add to the purée of apples, and serve with cream.

APPLES FRIED.

Wash and wipe some tart cooking apples, cut in slices a quarter of an inch thick, core and fry them in butter until tender and brown, dredge them with sugar and serve hot.

APPLE MARMALADE.

Two pounds of tart cooking apples, one pound of sugar, one pint of water, one lemon and some blanched almonds. Stir the sugar and water together and boil it until it strings from the spoon, then add the apples pared and cored and cut in small pieces, cook until very thick, flavor with the juice and grated peel of a small lemon. Turn into a wet mould, when cold set on the ice. Turn out on a glass dish, stick it thickly over with the blanched almonds, garnish with whipped cream and serve with cream.

APPLE MERINGUE.

Put a pint of apple sauce, made of tart cooking apples, slightly sweetened, into a pudding dish. Beat the whites of four eggs to a stiff froth and stir into it a cup and a quarter of sugar, flavor with a very little extract of lemon—a few drops only—and spread over the apple sauce, and bake twenty or twenty-five minutes. Make a custard of the four egg yolks and a pint of milk, sweeten to taste and flavor with vanilla. Serve the meringue very cold in the dish in which it is baked, with the custard as a sauce in a sauceboat or glass pitcher.

APPLE PUDDING.—No. 1.

Take some tart cooking apples, pare, core and slice them and lay in cold water for a few minutes to prevent them from turning dark. Put the apples in a porcelain lined or granite saucepan and add water as deep as the apples, but not to cover them. Cover the saucepan tightly and let the apples cook until tender, then mash well, add sugar, grated lemon peel and cinnamon to taste. Put it back on the stove, and when it comes to a boil add a tablespoonful of potato flour mixed with a little cold water, stir well and let it cook for a few minutes. Turn it into a mould and serve the next day with cream.

APPLE PUDDING.—No. 2.

Prepare the apples as for Apple Pudding, No. 1. When tender mash through a colander, and put the purée back on the stove. When it boils stir in a very heaping tablespoonful of potato flour mixed with a little cold water, and let it cook for a few minutes. Remove from the fire, stir in a wine glass of sherry. Turn into a mould, set it on the ice until the next day and serve with cream.

APPLES STEWED IN BUTTER.

Take half a dozen good, tart cooking apples—greenings or Newtown pippins; peel, cut in slices about a quarter of an inch thick and core them. Melt an ounce of butter in a spider, and lay in the slices of apples with a quarter of a pound of granula-

ted sugar and the juice of a lemon, stew gently over a
moderate fire. When done arrange them nicely on
a dish, melt a generous tablespoonful of currant jelly
in the spider, and when ready to serve mix with it
half a glass of Madeira or sherry; pour over the
apples and serve.

TO STEAM APPLES.

Pare and core some good cooking apples, place
them in an earthen or granite ware dish that fits in
a steamer. Have water boiling in the steamer, set
the dish over it, stretch a towel over the top, put on
the cover and fold the ends of the towel over it.
Steam the apples until tender—about twenty minutes. Take the apples out, measure the juice in the
pan and add to it an equal quantity of sugar, flavor
with a little lemon juice, cook until thick, put the
apples in a glass dish and pour the syrup over them.
It will be a jelly when cold. Serve with cream.

SCALLOPED APPLES.

Pare, core and cut in slices some good, tart cooking apples, put a layer in a baking dish with sugar,
cinnamon and a grating of lemon rind, dot with tiny
lumps of butter, then another layer of apples, sugar,
etc., and so on until the dish is full. Add a very little
water and the juice of a lemon, and use a little more
sugar and butter on top than on the other layers.
Bake until the apples are thoroughly cooked. Cover
until nearly done, when the cover should be removed
to allow them to brown. Serve hot with cream or
hard sauce.

BANANA FRITTERS.

Half a pint of sweet milk, a scant half pint of
flour, two rounded teaspoonfuls of baking powder
and a small pinch of salt, stir all together; this
should make a batter as thick as that of cake. Roll
the pieces of fruit in it with a fork, and drop quickly

into boiling fat. The batter should be prepared just as it is wanted and not allowed to stand. Cut three medium-sized bananas into three pieces each and divide each slice lengthwise so that the fruit will be thin enough to cook thoroughly while the batter is browning. This recipe will make eighteen small fritters. Put them on a hot platter—do not pile up—and serve immediately with a fruit sauce.

BAVARIAN CHERRY CAKE.

Half a pound of fine, juicy black cherries, five tablespoonfuls of fine bread crumbs, five tablespoonfuls of powdered sugar, five eggs and one ounce of sweet chocolate grated. Put the grated chocolate in a mixing bowl, break an egg into it and add one tablespoonful of bread crumbs and one of sugar, beat light and break another egg into it, adding another tablespoonful of bread crumbs and one of sugar. Then separate the three remaining eggs, the yolks from the whites, adding one yolk at a time alternately with bread crumbs and sugar until all are used. Add the cherries. Beat the three whites of eggs to a stiff froth and fold it in lightly. Butter thick a cake mould, sift dried bread crumbs over it, turn the cake into it and bake about three-quarters of an hour in a moderate oven. Test it as other cake. In Bavaria it is served cold, but I think it would also be nice hot with fruit sauce.

CRANBERRY BAVARIAN CREAM.

Stew one quart of cranberries; while hot rub through a sieve; measure out half a pint, and add to it a half cup of granulated sugar. Have a quarter of a box of gelatine soaked in a quarter of a cup of water one hour, set the bowl over steam entirely to dissolve the gelatine, then add the cranberries. Turn it into an earthenware bowl, set in a pan of ice water and beat until it is perfectly cold and begins to thicken, then add half a cup of rich milk and beat again, and at the last add half a cup of whipped cream. Beat it thoroughly and turn it into a mould and set on the ice to congeal. Serve with cream. Do not use a tin mould for cranberries.

A MOULD OF FRESH FRUIT.

Take enough fresh, ripe currants and raspberries to make half a cupful of juice of each, and press through a sieve fine enough to retain the seeds; or the fruit may be strained and squeezed through cheese cloth. Take also enough ripe cherries to make a cupful of juice and mix all together. Put a quart of boiling water in a saucepan over the fire with four ounces of sugar and two ounces of almonds blanched and cut fine. Mix five ounces of arrowroot or the same quantity of potato flour with the cold fruit juices, stir it into the boiling water and let it boil about five minutes, turn it into a wet mould, and when cold set on the ice. This should be made the day before it is to be served. Serve with cream.

A DESSERT OF MIXED FRUIT.

Peel some sweet, juicy oranges, removing all the white, bitter skin, cut in thin slices and put a layer at the bottom of a glass dish, sprinkle with sugar, then put a layer of freshly grated cocoanut and a layer of bananas, cut in thin slices, and repeat, beginning again with oranges, until the bowl is full, finishing with a layer of cocoanut. Pour over it any juice that may have run from the oranges, and if liked a glass or two of sherry may be added. Serve very cold.

GOOSEBERRY PUDDING.

Use either ripe or unripe English gooseberries for this pudding, stem and pick off the flower, wash and cover with water and cook until tender, strain through a sieve. Return to the fire, let it come to a boil, sweeten to taste, flavor with cinnamon and some almonds blanched and cut fine. Stiffen with potato flour as in other fruit puddings—a tablespoonful to a quart of the purée—and mould and serve in the same way.

PINEAPPLE MERINGUE.

Half a large or one small pineapple grated, two ounces of butter, three of granulated sugar, an ounce and a half of grated bread crumbs, the yolks of three eggs and the whites of four. Cream the butter and sugar, add the yolks and one white of egg beaten well together, then the fruit and bread crumbs; turn into a pudding dish and bake twenty minutes. Beat three whites of eggs to a stiff froth and add three-quarters of a cup of granulated sugar to it, flavor with a few drops of almond extract, spread over the pudding, set the dish in a pan of warm water in the oven and bake about ten or fifteen minutes. Test with a straw; when it comes out clean it is done. Serve cold.

PRUNE SOUFFLÉ.

Soak three-quarters of a pound of prunes in water to cover them over night, cook until soft in the water they were soaked in, drain, take out the stones and press through a purée sieve. Add half a cup of granulated sugar and the whites of three eggs beaten to a stiff froth. Bake in a pudding dish twenty minutes. Serve in the dish in which it is baked, cold, with cream.

PRUNE MOULD.

Prepare a prune purée as above and to the same quantity have a third of a box of gelatine soaked in a little of the water the prunes were cooked in, and dissolved over the teakettle. Stir quickly into the purée, then add three whites of eggs beaten to a stiff froth. Wet a mould and pour the mixture into it;

set on the ice to congeal. Turn out on a glass dish and serve with cream.

STEWED DRIED FIGS.

Wash and cut in half two dozen dried figs, slice very thin one small lemon, add to the figs, put in a saucepan and pour over them cold water almost to cover. Let them cook until the lemon is clear. Sweeten to taste.

RHUBARB MERINGUE.

Take three cups of stewed rhubarb, put in a saucepan over the fire, sweeten to taste, and when hot add two ounces of butter and three ounces of bread crumbs dried and rolled fine, the juice and rind of half a lemon. Remove from the fire and stir in three egg yolks, turn it into a pudding dish, set aside while preparing the meringue. Beat the whites of three eggs to a stiff froth, add three-quarters of a cup of granulated sugar and pour over the rhubarb. Set the pudding dish in a pan of hot water in the oven and bake ten or fifteen minutes. Test with a broom straw; when it comes out of the meringue clean it is done. Serve cold with cream.

SCALLOPED RHUBARB.

A dozen large stalks of young rhubarb, washed and scraped and cut in thin slices, half a loaf of bakers' stale bread grated, four heaping tablespoonfuls of granulated sugar, one generous tablespoonful of butter, and the grated rind of a large lemon. Butter a pudding dish, divide the ingredients into four parts, begin with the rhubarb and finish with bread crumbs. Sprinkle the sugar and grated lemon peel over the rhubarb and cut the butter in tiny bits over the bread crumbs, dredge the top with sugar. Bake three-quarters of an hour in a moderate oven and serve hot with cream or hard sauce.

RICE AND DATE PUDDING.

Half a cup of rice washed and boiled in water, one pound of dates, washed first in cold then in hot water, stoned and chopped a little, one pint of milk, two eggs, two tablespoonfuls of granulated sugar, and a little salt. Butter well a pudding dish, lay in half the dates, then over them half the rice, then dates again with a layer of rice on top. Beat the eggs light, add to them the milk, sugar and salt, and pour over the rice and fruit and bake from twenty-five to thirty minutes. Serve cold, with cream.

RICE AND FIG PUDDING

may be made according to the preceding recipe, steaming or stewing the figs a little and chopping slightly.

RICE AND RAISIN PUDDING.

Soak the raisins, seed them and stew a little, and follow the same recipe.

RICE AND PRUNE PUDDING.

Soak the prunes over night, stew and stone and slightly chop them and proceed as in the other puddings. Any kind of dried or fresh fruit may be used for this very wholesome and nutritious pudding.

RICE FLOUR PUDDING.

Take a quart of milk, leaving out enough to mix with three ounces of rice flour, put the rest in a saucepan over the fire. When it boils add one ounce and a half of sugar, one-half ounce of sweet and a few bitter almonds, blanched and pounded, or chopped very fine, one ounce of butter, and a small piece of vanilla bean if convenient, if not flavor at the last with vanilla extract. Mix the three ounces of rice flour with milk, reserved from the quart, and stir into the pudding. Beat one egg yolk with half a cup of cream and stir in just before removing from the fire. Turn into a mould that has been dipped in cold water and serve very cold with fruit sauce.

RICE SOUFFLÉ COLD.

Put into a double boiler a quarter of a pound of well washed rice, a pint and a third of milk, a small tablespoonful of butter, and cook until the rice is so stiff that it no longer adheres to the sides of the pan. Soak a heaping tablespoonful of gelatine in two tablespoonfuls of water fifteen minutes. Put a pint of thin cream or rich milk in a saucepan over the fire with two ounces of blanched and pounded almonds; while it is coming to a boil beat two egg yolks and two tablespoonfuls of granulated sugar together until light, then add the gelatine to the milk on the stove. When it has dissolved pour a little of the cream into the eggs and sugar, mix well, then turn it back into the saucepan, and stir all rapidly together until it begins to thicken, remove at once from the fire, add to the rice and beat until smooth. Rinse a mould with cold water, turn the soufflé into it and set on ice until it is wanted. Turn it out on a glass dish and serve with or without a fruit sauce.

RICE PUDDING.—No. 1.

Take a quarter of a pound of rice, wash well in cold and then scald in boiling water, drain and put on in a quart of sweet milk in a double boiler, cook one hour and a half. A little before it is done stir in an ounce and a half of butter, one ounce of sugar, a little grated lemon peel, a few sweet and bitter almonds blanched and chopped very fine or pounded in a mortar. Don't stir too much, but keep the rice grains whole. When done dip a mould in cold water and turn the rice into it. Set it on the ice and serve very cold with a fruit sauce.

RICE PUDDING.—No. 2.

Put a scant half cup of rice to soak in water for an hour, then boil in salted boiling water for twenty minutes. While it is cooking put three cups of rich milk and half a cup of sugar in a saucepan on the stove, mix a tablespoonful of corn starch with a little cold milk, stir with the milk and sugar and let it come to a boil, then add a cupful of the hot boiled rice and stir until it thickens like custard. Turn it into a pudding dish, flavor with vanilla or anything liked and bake slowly until a delicate brown. Serve cold in the dish in which it is baked, with brandy peaches or any fruit liked.

RICE OMELETTE SOUFFLE.

Boil a quarter of a pound of well-washed Carolina rice in a pint and a half of milk until stiff. Stir in two ounces of butter, half a pint of cream and four egg yolks beaten light with two ounces of granulated sugar and vanilla to taste, add a quarter of a pound of citron cut fine and two ounces of almonds blanched and pounded fine in a mortar. Stir all well together, adding at the last four whites of eggs beaten very stiff. Put in a pudding dish and bake until firm— about half an hour. Serve immediately in the dish in which it was baked.

STRAWBERRY SHORTCAKE.—No. 1.

Puff paste makes a delicious strawberry short-cake. Roll thin, as for pie crust, and line three layer cake tins and bake. Put a quart of fresh, ripe strawberries stemmed in a bowl, sweeten them, cover and stand the bowl on the shelf over the range, stir occasionally and mash slightly with the back of a spoon. When serving time comes lay one of the shells on the dish in which it is to be served, and pour a third of the berries over it, then put on a second and a third, decorate the top layer with whipped cream and serve with cream. It should be served immediately after the berries are added to the crust that it may be crisp. Both berries and shells should be cold.

STRAWBERRY SHORTCAKE.—No. 2.

Make a biscuit dough in the proportion of a pint of flour, a heaping teaspoonful of baking powder and half a teaspoonful of salt, a tablespoonful of butter and enough milk to mix it. Roll about an inch thick, cut it round or oblong and bake in a quick oven about fifteen minutes. Cut around the edge and pull gently apart, butter slightly, have the berries prepared as for Shortcake No. 1. Put the crust on the serving dish, pour half the berries over it, put on the top and pour the remainder of the berries over it. Serve with cream.

LADIES' LOCKS FILLED WITH STRAWBERRIES.

Roll the puff paste thin, cut in strips an inch wide and about twelve inches long; wind these around the forms overlapping the paste as it is wound. Brush over with beaten egg and bake on the forms. When baked slip the forms out, fill with strawberries prepared as for strawberry shortcake.

STRAWBERRIES SCALLOPED.

Equal quantities of fresh strawberries and bakers' stale bread grated. Begin with a layer of the berries, sprinkle well with sugar, then a layer of bread crumbs, dot with bits of butter, then another layer of fruit and sugar; finish with bread crumbs and butter, sprinkle a little sugar over the top and bake half an hour in a good oven. Serve hot with cream. Currants and raspberries, either separately or mixed, and blackberries also make excellent puddings.

CURRANT PUDDING.

Stem and wash some currants, mash through a sieve, add as much water as there is currant juice and sweeten to taste. To one quart of liquid take two ounces of Groult's potato flour. Mix the potato flour with a little of the cold fruit juice, put the rest over the fire, and when it comes to a boil stir in the flour and let it cook for a few minutes. It will become clear. Turn it into a mould that has been dipped in cold water, and set it when cool on the ice until the next day. Turn out carefully and serve with cream.

STEWED DATES.

Break the dates apart, wash in cold, then in hot water, drain them and cover with cold water; cook until tender—a very few minutes—take out the fruit, add a little sugar to the water and boil five minutes, pour over the dates and set away to get cold.

STUFFED DATES.

Wash the dates as in the other recipes, drain in a colander and shake from time to time until they are dry. Stone them and fill with blanched almonds, or chopped nuts or cocoanut grated.

TAPIOCA AND APPLE PUDDING.

Six good, tart cooking apples, three-quarters of a cup of pearl tapioca, sugar to taste and one quart of water. Soak the tapioca in the water two hours, then put in a double boiler and cook until clear, sweeten to taste. It may be flavored with the rind of lemon cut very thin and removed when the tapioca is done. Peel and core the apples and fill the holes with sugar, arrange them in a pudding dish and pour the tapioca over them, bake until the apples are tender. A few tiny bits of butter on the top will make it brown a little. Serve hot or cold with cream and sugar.

TAPIOCA AND STRAWBERRY JELLY.

Five ounces of Groult's tapioca, two cups of boiling water, two cups of strawberry juice, four heaping tablespoonfuls of sugar and a dash of salt. Hull and wash the berries, mash with a spoon and strain through a fine cheese-cloth. Put the boiling water in a double boiler, and sprinkle in the tapioca, stirring to prevent lumping. Let it cook until clear, add the sugar and salt, and then the strawberry juice, and boil until thick—a few minutes only; turn into an earthenware mould; when cold set on the ice. It is better to make it the day before it is wanted. It should be served with cream.

TAPIOCA AND RASPBERRY JELLY.

Follow the above recipe, using raspberries in the same proportion.

TAPIOCA AND CURRANT JELLY.

Follow the recipe for tapioca and strawberry jelly.

PEARL SAGO AND FRUIT JELLIES.

Soak half a cup of pearl sago two hours in a cup of cold water, then add half a cup of water and a cup and a half of fruit juice—strawberry, raspberry, or currant; boil for twenty minutes and sweeten to taste. Fruit syrups may be used in winter; it will require less of the syrup than fruit juice.

BREAD AND BUTTER PUDDING.—No. 1.

Cut six small tea buns in half, butter well, using two generous ounces of butter for the six, and put them together again. Beat three eggs with a cup and a half of rich milk, add half a cup of almonds blanched and chopped fine, one ounce of sugar, two tablespoonfuls of sherry, let the buns soak in this for awhile. Butter a mould, sprinkle with fine bread crumbs, take the buns out of the custard, lay them in the mould and pour the custard over them. Set the mould in a pan of boiling water in the oven and bake three-quarters of an hour, and serve hot with a sauce.

BREAD AND BUTTER PUDDING.—No. 2.

Cut some slices of home-made bread about half an inch thick, butter and lay in a pudding dish, sprinkle with currants, put another layer of buttered bread and currants. Beat three eggs light and stir into a pint of milk, sweeten to taste, flavor with a little grated lemon peel or cinnamon, pour over the bread and butter and bake in a moderate oven until the custard is set. Test with a knife; if it comes out clean it is done. If baked too long the pudding will be watery. Serve cold and in the dish in which it is baked.

BREAD CUSTARD.

Put a pint of rich milk in a saucepan on the fire. When it comes to a boil, add half a cup of grated stale bread crumbs, then stir in a heaping table-spoonful of butter, a little grating of lemon peel, a quarter of a cup of granulated sugar and a table-spoonful of almonds blanched and chopped fine. Have two eggs beaten light, remove the saucepan from the fire, stir a little of the mixture into the eggs and then turn that into the saucepan, stir well for a moment and pour it into a pudding dish. Set the dish in a pan of hot water in the oven and bake about twenty minutes, until firm in the center; test with a knife. If it comes out clean the pudding is done; if it bakes too long it will be watery. It may be eaten cold or hot. If served hot add a quarter of a cup more bread crumbs.

FRIED BREAD.

Sweeten a pint of milk, flavor with cinnamon or nutmeg to taste. Have some slices of home-made bread half an inch thick, cut off the crust and soak the bread in the custard until all is absorbed, turning the bread in it. Put some butter in a spider; when hot fry the bread a nice brown on both sides. Arrange the slices nicely on a platter and serve with or without a sauce.

CHOCOLATE CREAM.

Soak a third of a box of gelatine in a very little cold water. Put a cup and a half of milk in a saucepan with four ounces of sweet, fine chocolate grated, let it boil until dissolved and add a slightly heaping tablespoonful of sugar. Take two-thirds of the soaked gelatine and put into the chocolate when melted, cool the mixture and turn into a mould, roll the mould from side to side in the hands until it is thoroughly coated with the mixture about a finger thick. When cold, even off the surface with a knife. Whip about half a pint of nice, rich cream, sweeten with powdered sugar and flavor with vanilla. Melt the other third of the soaked gelatine in a little boiling water and stir quickly into the cream and fill the chocolate with it. Set on the ice. Serve very cold.

CHOCOLATE CUSTARD.

Put a pint and a half of rich milk into a double boiler over the fire with the third of a vanilla bean split and cut in small pieces, let it come to a boil, and stir in two ounces of fine, sweet chocolate grated and a lump of butter the size of a walnut. Let it boil for a few moments, remove from the fire and beat very light four eggs, strain the chocolate gradually over them, stirring all the time, add a little salt, and sugar if necessary. Rinse a plain mould in cold water, pour the custard into it, set the mould in a pan of hot water and bake twenty-five minutes. Test with a knife. Too long cooking makes the custard watery. It must be served ice cold and may be prepared the day before. Serve with cream or soft boiled custard.

CHOCOLATE PUDDING.

Beat one-quarter of a pound of butter to a cream and stir in six egg yolks, one at a time, then add a quarter of a pound of fine, sweet chocolate grated, a cup of almonds blanched and chopped fine, six tablespoonfuls of granulated sugar and one tablespoonful of citron cut very fine, beat the six whites of eggs to a stiff froth and stir in at the last. Pour into a mould and boil three-quarters of an hour and send to the table hot with whipped cream poured around it, or any fine sauce served in a sauceboat.

COTTAGE PUDDING.

One cup of granulated sugar, a cup and a half of flour sifted, half a cup of milk, a heaping tablespoonful of butter, two eggs, whites and yolks beaten separately, a teaspoonful of Cleveland's baking powder mixed with the flour. Beat butter and sugar to a cream, add the well-beaten yolks of the eggs, then add milk and flour alternately by degrees, and the whites of eggs beaten to a stiff froth, stirred in at the last. Bake half an hour. Serve hot with plenty of sauce.

CARAMEL CUSTARD BAKED.

A pint and a half of rich milk, a cup and a half of granulated sugar, the fourth of a vanilla bean. Put the milk and vanilla bean cut small into a double boiler over the fire. Melt the sugar without water in a spider, stirring constantly until it is all dissolved and the syrup is a rich golden brown. Do not let it get too dark or it will be bitter. When the milk is at the boiling point stir in half the boiling syrup—if put in too fast the milk will boil over. Let it cook until the sugar (if it hardened as it touched the milk) dissolves. Have four eggs beaten very light in a bowl, pour the milk over them, add a little salt, and if vanilla bean is not used for flavoring, stir in extract of vanilla to taste. Rinse a mould with cold water, pour the custard into it and set it in a pan of hot water in the oven, bake from twenty to twenty-five minutes and test with a knife. If it comes out clean it is done. Add boiling water to the remainder of the syrup and let it cook gently until it is the consistency of thick cream. Flavor with vanilla. Serve very cold.

SOFT-BOILED CUSTARD.

Put a quart of rich milk in a double boiler over the fire with a third of a vanilla bean, split in half, and sugar to taste. Beat the whites of six eggs to a stiff froth, add three heaping teaspoonfuls of granulated sugar, and when the milk comes to the boiling point drop the whites of eggs into it by tablespoonfuls in egg-shape, turn them over in the hot milk for a few seconds, repeat until all are done, drain them and return the milk to the saucepan. Beat the six egg yolks to a light cream, turn the hot milk over it gradually and pour the custard back into the boiler; return to the fire and stir vigorously until it thickens and is smooth to the taste. Remove from the fire, pour at once into a bowl, add a little salt, and set aside to cool. Then put on the ice and at serving time turn into a glass bowl, arrange the whites of eggs on top and serve with sponge cake.

A SIMPLE DESSERT.

A loaf of stale sponge cake—one that has been baked in a border mould looks pretty. Saturate the cake with orange juice to which has been added a little lemon. Stick the cake over with blanched almonds and fill the center with whipped cream. If the cake is a plain loaf, pile the cream around it.

GINGER CREAM.

Soak a quarter of a box of gelatine in half a cup of milk for half an hour, then place the bowl over steam until the gelatine is perfectly dissolved. Add to it four ounces of granulated sugar and a pint of whipped cream, two tablespoonfuls of preserved ginger chopped fine, two tablespoonfuls of the ginger syrup and a tablespoonful of almonds blanched and chopped very fine. Stir until it begins to thicken, pour into a mould and set on the ice. Serve in a glass dish and powder the top with chopped almonds.

GRAHAM PUDDING.

Two cups of Graham flour, one cup of milk, one cup of Porto Rico molasses, one cup of raisins stoned and slightly chopped, one egg, one even teaspoonful of soda, one teaspoonful of ground cinnamon, one-half teaspoonful of cloves, a little nutmeg, if liked, and a small pinch of salt. Flour the raisins with a little white flour, mix all the ingredients thoroughly together, butter a mould and steam three hours. Serve with a sauce. If there should be any of the pudding left over, it can be used by cutting in slices half an inch thick, each piece dipped in milk, in which an egg has been stirred, fried brown in a little butter, and served hot with a sauce.

NALESNEKY (a Russian Recipe).

Beat three yolks of eggs light, add to it half a cup of milk, half a cup of water, one cup of flour, and a little salt, mix until smooth, then stir in the whites of three eggs beaten to a stiff froth. Have some melted butter, brush over the bottom of a frying pan and pour a little of the batter into it, let it cover the bottom of the pan without being thicker than paper, let it brown, turning it to brown the other side, spread with any jelly preferred, fold in half and fold again, making a wedge-shaped cake. Use all the batter in this way, and serve hot. It would be well to have two spiders in use.

NOODLE PUDDING.

Put two ounces and a half of noodles in a pint of boiling milk and cook until stiff like mush. Remove from the fire, and stir in one ounce and a half of butter, one ounce of sugar, two tablespoonfuls of finely chopped almonds, a few drops of extract of almond, when cool add three eggs and a quarter of a cup of cream beaten together, and turn the mixture into a well buttered mould sprinkled thoroughly with fine sifted bread crumbs. Set the mould in a pan of boiling water in the oven, cover to prevent browning, and if the mould has a pipe through the center bake half an hour, if a plain mould it will require three-quarters of an hour. Turn out of the mould and serve hot with a sauce.

PARADISE PUDDING.

Melt two and a half ounces of butter in a saucepan, stir into it a quarter of a pound of sifted flour and a cup and a half of cream or rich milk, let it cook until it no longer sticks to the side of the pan, remove from the fire and let it cool. Then stir in an ounce and a half of sugar, three heaping tablespoonfuls of almonds blanched and chopped and a little vanilla to flavor—vanilla sugar is better than the extract—then mix in five well beaten eggs, a little at a time. Turn it into a well buttered mould sprinkled with dried and sifted bread crumbs, set in a pan of hot water in the oven, cover to prevent browning and bake about three-quarters of an hour. Serve hot with a wine or fruit sauce.

PRINCESS PUDDING.

Melt two and a half ounces of butter in a quarter of a cup of rich milk over the fire, stir an ounce and a half of flour into half a cup of milk and add to the boiling milk, stirring constantly until it becomes a smooth paste and no longer adheres to the pan. Remove from the fire; when cold stir in one good ounce of sugar, an ounce of almonds blanched and pounded very fine with a dozen cardamom seeds, three well beaten eggs, a little at a time, half a teaspoonful of almond extract. Beat well, turn into a buttered pudding mould sprinkled with fine bread crumbs, set the mould covered in a pan of boiling water in the oven, and if the mould has a pipe in the center bake from thirty to thirty-five minutes. Turn it out and serve immediately with a fruit or wine sauce.

ENGLISH PLUM PUDDING.

Two pounds of raisins, one pound of currants, one pound of citron, half a pound of almonds, one pound of butter, one pound of flour, one pound of brown sugar, one teaspoonful each of ground cinnamon, cloves, allspice, ginger and nutmeg, half a pint of brandy and wine mixed and one dozen eggs. Boil six hours. Keep water boiling by the side of pudding boiler all the time and continually refill as the water evaporates. In preparing the pudding have all the fruit stoned and cut, but not too fine, the almonds blanched and chopped. Incorporate all the ingredients well together before adding the eggs and spirits and beat the mixture well together for at least an hour—the longer the better.

SAGO SOUFFLÉ.

A pint of rich milk, two and a half ounces of butter, one ounce and a half of sugar, two ounces of pearl sago, one ounce and a half of blanched almonds chopped very fine. Mix all together, put over the fire and let it cook for fifteen minutes, stirring constantly, remove from the stove and let it cool. Beat three eggs and add a little at a time until all is used, flavor with half a teaspoonful of almond extract, put in a pudding dish and bake half an hour. Sift a little powdered sugar over it and serve immediately in the dish in which it is baked.

SEMOULINA PUDDING.

Put a pint and a half of milk on the fire to boil with two ounces of butter, three ounces of sugar, an ounce and a half of sweet and two or three bitter almonds blanched and chopped very fine, sprinkle into it three ounces of semoulina or farina, and boil until quite stiff, stirring constantly. Remove from the fire and turn into a mould that has been wet in cold water. Serve very cold with fruit sauce or cream.

SERNIKY (a Russian Recipe).

Put one ball of pot cheese, such as is sold at a creamery for five cents, in a mixing bowl, break it up with a spoon, and add to it a heaping tablespoonful of butter, the well beaten yolks of four eggs, a little salt, a heaping dessertspoonful of currants and two slightly heaping tablespoonfuls of flour. Mix all well together and let it stand an hour or more. Sprinkle a pastry board thickly with flour, turn the mixture out from the bowl, cut off pieces of it and roll with the hands until about an inch and a half thick, cut in pieces about two inches long, the ends bias. Have a saucepan ready with boiling water, drop the pieces into this without crowding and cook until they float—about five minutes—take them out with a skimmer. Roll in dried bread crumbs, fry brown on both sides in butter, and serve hot with cream and sugar.

STEAMED PUDDING.

One cup of raisins stoned and chopped, one cup of butter chopped, two cups and a half of flour, one cup of Porto Rico molasses, one cup of sweet milk, a scant teaspoonful of soda, a teaspoonful of cinnamon, and a little nutmeg. Steam in a mould two hours. Serve hot with a sauce.

SPONGE CAKE MERINGUE.

Butter well a pudding dish, cover the bottom with slices of stale sponge cake about an inch thick, fit closely together. Beat the yolks of three eggs with three teaspoonfuls of granulated sugar, add the grated rind of half and the juice of one orange, the juice of half a small lemon, two tablespoonfuls of melted butter and stir in soda as large as a pea into a cup and a half of milk, add this to the orange and egg and stir well together. Pour three-quarters of this mixture over the cake, set the dish in a pan of boiling water in the oven, and when the cake has absorbed the custard and no longer floats, add the remainder of the custard. While the pudding is baking make a meringue of three whites of eggs beaten to a stiff froth and three-quarters of a cup of granulated sugar, flavor with the grated rind of half an orange and a few drops of orange extract. Spread quickly over the pudding and bake fifteen minutes.

PUDDING OF STALE CAKE.

Almost any kind of stale cake will do for this pudding. To three cups of the cake crumbs allow a cup and a half of milk, three tablespoonfuls of melted butter and two eggs beaten light. Pour the milk over the crumbs and let them soak until soft, then stir in the melted butter and the eggs, beat well and pour into a mould that has been well buttered and sprinkled with fine bread crumbs. Set the mould in a pan of hot water in the oven, cover to prevent browning and bake three-quarters of an hour. Serve hot with fruit or wine sauce.

BAKED TAPIOCA PUDDING.

Soak a cup and a half of pearl tapioca two hours in a quart of rich milk, put it in a double boiler and cook until the tapioca looks clear, remove from the fire, stir into it two slightly heaping tablespoonfuls of butter and a scant half cup of sugar. When cold add four eggs beaten light and flavor with vanilla, or the rind of a lemon grated and added when the tapioca is cooking. Butter a mould, sprinkle with dried bread crumbs, turn the mixture into it and bake. Turn out on a platter and serve hot with a foaming sauce.

TAPIOCA CREAM.

A quarter of a cup of pearl tapioca, a cup of water, a pint of rich milk, three even tablespoonfuls of sugar, a teaspoonful of vanilla extract, two eggs and a little salt. Soak the tapioca in the water two hours, then turn it into a double boiler with the milk; when it boils, beat the yolks of eggs to a cream and the whites to a stiff froth, mix a little of the milk with the egg, then pour it into the boiler and stir a moment until thick, remove from the fire, add the vanilla extract and stir in lightly the beaten whites of eggs. The froth should show through the custard. Serve very cold in a glass bowl.

STEAMED RICE.

Half a cup of rice, half a teaspoonful of salt and one and one-third cups of boiling water. Put in small cups in a steamer, cover closely and steam three-quarters of an hour. Serve with stewed fruit and cream or sugar and cream.

RICE CAKE.

Four ounces of rice, a pint and a half of milk, six eggs, two ounces and a half of sugar, half a cup of almonds blanched and chopped, two ounces of stoned raisins, a little citron, three heaping tablespoonfuls of dried bread crumbs, and four ounces of butter. Wash the rice and scald with boiling water, drain and put it into the milk, which must be boiling on the stove, cook until it is stiff like mush; remove from the fire and stir into it the butter. When it is cool, add the eggs, one at a time, the sugar, the almonds chopped fine, the raisins, a little citron finely cut, and the bread crumbs dried and rolled fine. Butter a mould, turn the cake into it and bake one hour in a moderate oven. Serve cold.

BROWN BREAD PUDDING.

Put in a bowl the yolks of four eggs and three whole eggs and six and a half ounces of sugar; beat together for fifteen minutes, then add six and a half ounces of almonds blanched and chopped fine, a dash of cinnamon, a tablespoonful of chocolate and four even tablespoonfuls of citron cut very fine; then add eight ounces and a half of brown bread grated and soaked in a few spoonfuls of claret or milk. Butter a mould, sprinkle with bread crumbs, pour the pudding into it and set it in a pan of hot water in a moderate oven. Bake three-quarters of an hour and serve with a sauce.

Ices.

VANILLA ICE CREAM.

A quart of rich milk, three-quarters of a pound of sugar, eight egg yolks and a small vanilla bean. Put the milk in a double boiler with the vanilla bean split into halves; beat the sugar and eggs to a cream, stir into the hot milk and beat briskly until thick, remove from the fire, strain; when cold, freeze.

COFFEE ICE CREAM.

A quart of rich milk, three-quarters of a pound of sugar, five ounces of coffee, eight egg yolks. Grind the coffee and stir it into half a pint of boiling milk, set it one side; put the rest of the milk in a double boiler, beat the eggs and sugar together until light, stir into the hot milk, stir briskly until it thickens, add the milk and coffee, turn it into a bowl and let it stand until the last moment; strain and freeze.

STRAWBERRY ICE CREAM.

A pint of cream, a pint of strawberry purée and three-quarters of a pound of sugar. Mix the sugar and strawberry purée together and let it stand until the sugar is dissolved, then add the cream; pass it through a sieve and freeze.

RASPBERRY ICE CREAM.

Follow the recipe for strawberry ice cream, using a little less sugar. All kinds of fresh fruit purées may be used for ice creams.

WALNUT ICE CREAM.

Follow the recipe for vanilla ice cream, adding a cup of English walnuts chopped and pounded fine in a mortar, and a little salt. When cold, freeze.

ORANGE ICE.

Boil a quart of water and a pound of sugar together for ten minutes, skim and strain and set aside to get cold. Then add the juice of twelve oranges and two lemons, put in the freezer; when it commences to freeze stir in the whites of two eggs beaten to a stiff froth.

STRAWBERRY ICE.

One quart of berries, one pound of sugar and three-quarters of a pint of water. Sprinkle the sugar over the berries, stir well and mash with a wooden spoon, strain and press through a sieve, pouring the water over it gradually until all is used. Put into the freezer; when it begins to freeze the whites of two eggs beaten to a stiff froth may be added.

WHITE CURRANT ICE

may be made the same as orange ice, using a quart and a pint of currants, mashed and put through a sieve, and a quarter of a pound more sugar.

PINEAPPLE ICE.

One quart of water, a pound and a quarter of sugar boiled and skimmed as before, and the juice of one lemon and a large, perfectly ripe pineapple, carefully peeled and shredded fine with a silver fork; freeze.

LEMON ICE.

One quart of water, a pound and a quarter of sugar, the juice of six large, fine lemons. Prepare as before, adding the beaten whites of two eggs when it begins to freeze.

RASPBERRY ICE.

Follow the directions for strawberry ice, adding the juice of two lemons. Any ripe fruit may be used, such as peaches, apricots, plums and red currants, sweetening as they require.

FROZEN PUDDING.

Prepare a custard with a quart of rich milk, a pint of cream, a pound of sugar, and the yolks of eight eggs. Set it on the fire and stir constantly until it begins to thicken; remove from the fire, and when it is cold add three tablespoonfuls of brandy, one teaspoonful of vanilla, one teaspoonful of almond extract. Put in the freezer, and when partially frozen add a quarter of a pound of stoned raisins that have been cooked a little in water to soften them, a quarter of a pound of currants, a quarter of a pound of citron cut fine. Freeze smooth and put in a mould and pack in ice and salt.

WINDSOR ROCK PUNCH.

For twenty-four persons. Boil two quarts of cream; mix with it half a pound of granulated sugar and twelve eggs. Freeze the same as ice cream. Take one-half of the frozen mixture and add to it two wineglasses of Maraschino, one wineglass of Kirsch, and one-half wineglass of Santa Cruz rum; mix. When serving add a small lump of the frozen mixture to a punch glass of the other, or liquid.

Cakes.

CAKE MAKING.

Have all the ingredients measured or weighed, the pans lined with paper or oiled, the nuts or fruit prepared, and the flour sifted before beginning to make a cake. Sift the baking powder and cream of tartar and soda with the flour or a part of it. Use pastry flour for all cake. Never put all the milk into a cake batter by itself, as it curdles and makes a coarse grained cake, but stir it in alternately with the flour. Put all loaves of cake into a moderate oven, that they may rise before beginning to bake. After the cake rises the heat may be increased.

ANGEL CAKE.

The whites of nine large, fresh eggs. When they are partly beaten add one-half teaspoonful of cream of tartar and then finish beating—the cream of tartar makes them lighter—then add one and a quarter cups of granulated sugar, stir the sugar very lightly into the whites of the eggs, and add a teaspoonful of vanilla. Have flour sifted five times, measure a cupful and fold it in very carefully, not with a circular motion, and do not stir long. Turn it into a Turk's head mould and bake forty-five minutes. Do not grease the mould, and when taken out of the oven invert it until the cake is cold before removing from the pan. Never use a patent egg-beater for this cake, but a whip, taking long, rapid strokes, and make it in a large platter, not a bowl.

BERLINERKRANDS (a Norwegian Cake).

Half a pound of butter washed in two waters and beaten to a cream, two hard-boiled egg yolks mashed fine and stirred into two raw egg yolks, four ounces of powdered sugar stirred into the eggs, then mix all with the butter, add a pound of flour and a wineglass of brandy, mix well. Roll under the hand and make into small jumble cakes or krunchens. Beat the white of an egg, dip each cake into it and then roll in granulated sugar, bake a delicate brown in a very slow oven fifteen or twenty minutes. Grease the tins.

BLUEBERRY CAKE.

Half a cup of butter beaten to a cream with half a cup of sugar, one cup of Porto Rico molasses, one cup of thin sour cream or milk, three eggs, the whites and yolks beaten separately, two cups of berries, two and a half cups of flour, one teaspoonful of soda sifted with the flour. Bake as soft gingerbread and serve hot.

CINNAMON CAKE.

One cup of granulated sugar, butter the size of an egg, one egg, one cup of milk, two cups of flour, one teaspoonful of cream of tartar, half a teaspoonful of soda. Mix in the usual way, but sifting the soda and cream of tartar with the flour. Put in a shallow pan, sprinkle with sugar and cinnamon, and bake about fifteen minutes in a moderate oven.

CREAM PUFFS.

One pint of water, half a pound of butter, three-quarters of a pound of flour, and ten eggs. Boil the water and butter together, and while boiling stir in the flour. Let it boil five minutes, then stir in the eggs one at a time without beating. Drop into a pan by spoonfuls—not close together—and bake in a

quick oven fifteen minutes. When cold cut them open
and fill with the cream.

FILLING.—One quart of milk, two cups of sugar,
one cup of flour and four eggs. Boil the milk, beat
eggs, sugar and flour together and stir into the milk,
stir constantly until thick—about five minutes—and
flavor to taste.

LADY CAKE.

Half a cup of butter, one cup of granulated sugar,
half a cup of milk, two cups of flour, two teaspoonfuls of baking powder, the whites of four eggs, and a
teaspoonful of almond extract. Beat the butter and
sugar to a cream, stir the milk into one cup of the
flour and add to the butter and sugar, then the
whites of eggs beaten to a stiff froth. Sift the baking
powder and remaining cup of flour together, add to
the other ingredients with the teaspoonful of almond
extract. If baked in a loaf it will require three-quarters of an hour or more.

HONEY CAKE (a Norwegian Recipe).

Two pounds of strained honey, three-quarters of
a pound of light brown sugar, three-quarters of an
ounce of bicarbonate of potash, pounded very fine
and dissolved in a little water, one cup of cream, half
a cup of melted butter, ginger, cloves and pepper to
taste, stir this all well together, add to it as much
flour as will make it like a thick mush, set it away until the next day, then turn it into a well-greased cake
mould and bake about three-quarters of an hour.

SIMPLE FRUIT CAKE.

Three-quarters of a pound of butter, three-quarters of a pound of sugar, one pound of sifted flour,
one-half pound of currants washed, one-half pound of
raisins stoned and chopped, one-half pound of citron
cut fine, one teaspoonful each of cloves, mace, allspice,
cinnamon and nutmeg, one-half cup of milk, one-half

cup of brandy, four eggs and one teaspoonful of soda. Beat butter and sugar to a cream; add the yolks of eggs beaten light with the spices and brandy; then the fruit rolled in part of the flour; add the soda to the rest of the flour and stir alternately with the milk into the other ingredients; add at the last the whites of eggs beaten to a stiff froth. Bake two hours in a moderate oven.

BAVARIAN CAKE.

One-fifth of a pound of blanched and chopped almonds, one-fifth of a pound of flour, one-fifth of a pound of sugar, one-fifth of a pound of butter, two eggs, a saltspoonful of cinnamon, a saltspoonful of nutmeg. Put the flour in a mixing bowl, then the sugar and spices, the butter and almonds, break the two eggs over it all and beat with a spoon, form into a dough with the hands and roll out about an inch thick. Cut in any shape liked, either round, square or oblong, reserving a little for strips to decorate the top. Spread with jam, either currant or strawberry or raspberry, and lay the thin narrow strips of dough across the top. They should be cut with a jagging iron. Bake about three-quarters of an hour in a moderate oven.

POUND CAKE.

One cup of butter, a cup and a half of flour, a cup and a half of granulated sugar, six eggs, and half a teaspoonful of baking powder, flavor with almond extract or any flavoring to suit the taste. Beat the eggs together very light, then add sugar and beat again. Sift the flour and baking powder together, beat the butter to a cream, and stir the flour into it, and then add the eggs and sugar and flavoring.

SPONGE CAKE.—No. 1.

Twelve eggs, the weight of ten in powdered sugar, the weight of six in sifted flour, the grated rind and juice of one lemon. Beat the yolks of the eggs to a cream, add the sugar and stir well, and then the lemon juice and rind. Add the whites of eggs beaten to a stiff froth, and fold in the flour as quickly and lightly as possible.

SPONGE CAKE.—No. 2.

Four cups of flour, three cups of sugar, one cup of cold water, eight eggs, two even tablespoonfuls of baking powder, the grated peel of an orange. Pour the water on the sugar in a bowl, stir until almost dissolved, beat the whites to a stiff froth, the yolks to a cream, put one cup of flour with the yolks into the sugar and water, beat hard, add the whites of the eggs, mix the baking powder with the flour, and stir into the other ingredients by degrees quickly and lightly. Bake in a shallow pan in a quick oven. When it no longer sizzles it is done. Ice with a boiled icing while hot, flavored with almond extract.

CORN SPONGE CAKE (a Spanish Recipe).

Half a pound of corn meal, half a pound of butter, seven ounces of granulated sugar, seven eggs, two tablespoonfuls of catalan (brandy). Beat separately the whites and yolks of the eggs; when the yolks are beaten to a cream add the sugar, then the whites of eggs, stir the corn meal in lightly, then the butter melted, and the brandy. Mix well, pour into shallow pans well buttered, and bake in a moderate oven from twelve to fifteen minutes, test with a straw. Best when quite fresh.

SPICED GINGERBREAD.

One cup of Porto Rico molasses, one cup of boiling water, butter the size of an egg, half a teaspoonful of ground cloves, one teaspoonful of cinnamon, one egg, one teaspoonful of ginger, half a teaspoonful of soda, a light half pound of flour, a quarter of a cup of brown sugar. Melt the butter and stir into the molasses, add the spices, then the water. Sift the soda with the flour and add at the last. Currants and raisins stoned and chopped may be added and are an improvement. The cake may be baked in a loaf or in small moulds.

CREAM GINGERBREAD.

One cup of Porto Rico molasses, one cup of sour cream, two cups of sifted flour, one teaspoonful of salt, one teaspoonful of ginger, one even teaspoonful of soda, one egg, a little cinnamon, cloves and nutmeg, two tablespoonfuls of brown sugar. Beat the egg, sugar and spice together, add the molasses and one cup of flour, then the cream, after that the other cup of flour with the soda sifted together. It should be a thick batter, and if not thick enough add a little more flour—not more than half a cup. Bake in a shallow pan. When done the cake should be about two inches thick. Ice with boiled icing.

GINGER SPONGE CAKE.

Half a cup of milk, half a cup of molasses, one cup of sugar, a third of a cup of butter, a cup and a half of flour, half a teaspoonful of cream of tartar, a quarter of a teaspoonful of soda sifted together with the flour, two eggs, one teaspoonful of ginger, one teaspoonful of cinnamon, and half a teaspoonful of cloves. Bake in a shallow pan.

SOFT GINGERBREAD.

One cup of molasses, one cup of butter, one cup of brown sugar, one cup of sour milk, three and a half cups of flour, half a teaspoonful of soda, five eggs, ginger, allspice, cloves and cinnamon to taste. Beat butter and sugar to a cream, stir in the molasses and spice, add a cup of the flour, then part of the milk, mix the soda with the rest of the flour and stir in alternately with the milk. Bake in shallow pans in a moderate oven.

GINGER CAKES.

Three-quarters of a pound of butter, three-quarters of a pound of granulated sugar, one pound of flour, one teaspoonful of ginger, two even teaspoonfuls of soda sifted with the flour. Mix well together. Roll out, cut in small round cakes, brush over with white of egg, and sprinkle with sugar and finely chopped almonds. Bake in a slow oven.

GINGER SNAPS.—No. 1.

Rub three-quarters of a pound of butter into a pound of sifted flour and mix in half a pound of brown sugar, add six tablespoonfuls of ginger, one teaspoonful of powdered cloves, and two teaspoonfuls of cinnamon, stir in a pint of Porto Rico molasses and the grated peel of a large lemon, add at the last a teaspoonful of soda dissolved in tepid water. Beat the mixture hard with a wooden spoon, make it into a lump of dough just stiff enough to roll. Cut in small cakes and bake in a moderate oven.

GINGER SNAPS.—No. 2.

One pint of Porto Rico molasses, one pound of brown sugar, one pound of butter, two pounds of flour, two tablespoonfuls of ginger, two of cinnamon, half a tablespoonful of allspice, a teaspoonful of nutmeg and half an ounce of soda. Beat butter and sugar to a cream, add the spice and molasses, mix the soda with half of the flour and stir all together. Roll thin, cut in small cakes and bake in a moderate oven.

HARD GINGERBREAD.

Two cups of Porto Rico molasses, one cup of brown sugar, one cup of butter, two tablespoonfuls of ginger, flour to make the dough stiff enough to roll.

It requires to be kneaded thoroughly. It is better that the dough be made the day before the cakes are to be baked that it may dry a little, as they are spoiled if too much flour is added. Roll thin, cut in oblong cakes with a jagging iron, or in any way to suit the fancy.

BRANDY SNAPS.

One pound of flour, a quarter of a pound of butter, a quarter of a pound of brown sugar, three-quarters of a pound of maple syrup. Mix the ingredients well together and drop on greased paper; if it runs too much add flour, if not enough add more maple syrup.

PEPPER NUTS.—No. 1.

Two pounds of flour, one and a half pounds of sugar, half a pound of butter, three eggs, two even teaspoonfuls of soda sifted with the flour, pepper to taste. Beat the butter to a cream, add the sugar and beat very light, then the eggs and flour. Roll out and cut in small, round cakes, bake a light brown. They will keep a long time.

PEPPER NUTS—No. 2.

Half a pound of butter beaten to a cream, then add three-quarters of a pound of sugar, three egg yolks beaten light, half a cup of cream, two ounces of almonds chopped very fine, half a teaspoonful of almond extract, a little fine cut citron, and one pound of flour sifted with an even teaspoonful of soda. Mix well together, roll out and cut in small, round cakes and bake a light brown.

TEA CAKES.

One pint of cream, four heaping tablespoonfuls of granulated sugar, two eggs, a little cinnamon; beat well together and stir into it enough flour to roll. Roll out about a quarter of an inch thick, brush over with white of egg and sift sugar and cinnamon over it, cut into cakes about a finger long and one inch wide. Bake a delicate brown.

FIG CAKE.

Half a cup of butter, one cup of granulated sugar, half a cup of milk, two cups of flour, two rounded teaspoonfuls of baking powder, the whites of four eggs. Beat the butter and sugar to a cream, stir the milk and one cup of the flour together and add to the butter and sugar. Sift the remaining cup of flour and the baking powder together, beat the whites of egg to a stiff froth and stir alternately with the flour into the other ingredients. Grease three layer cake tins well, divide the batter evenly and bake from seven to ten minutes.

FILLING.—Boil without stirring until it is clear one cup of sugar wet with a little water; remove from the fire and stir into it three-quarters of a cup of figs chopped fine and a quarter of a cup of currants, washed and dried. Spread two of the layers with this, put them together and ice top and sides with a plain icing made as follows: The whites of two eggs beaten to a froth and one and a half cups of powdered sugar stirred into it and flavored with almond extract.

GINGER LAYER CAKE.

Two cups of flour, one cup of Porto Rico molasses, one cup of milk, the third of a cup of butter, one egg, one slightly heaping teaspoonful of soda sifted with the flour, one heaping teaspoonful of ginger, one cup of currants. Beat the egg a little, add the molasses with the butter melted and stirred into it, then the currants, about half the milk, all of the flour, beat well and add the rest of the milk. Bake in two cakes in a quick oven from twelve to fifteen minutes. Use the chocolate filling, given for chocolate layer cake, and ice the top and the sides with the same.

ORANGE CAKE.

Beat to a cream the yolks of four eggs with one cup of granulated sugar, to which add the whites of two eggs beaten to a stiff froth, one-half cup of milk alternately with one and a half cups of sifted flour into which a teaspoonful and a half of baking powder has been well mixed. Beat well and bake in three layers if the pans are large, or four if small, in a quick oven from seven to ten minutes, try with a broom straw, and when it comes out clean remove from the oven. Don't let them bake a moment too long, or they will not absorb the icing.

FILLING.—The whites of two eggs beaten to a stiff froth, to which add a cup of powdered sugar, pouring it in all at once and beating hard, then the grated rind of an orange—select one dark in color—and the juice. The mixture should be like a thick cream. Spread thickly on the cake while hot, and to what is left add enough sugar—about half a cupful—for frosting to harden. Ice the top and sides. This is a delicious cake, easily and quickly made.

PINEAPPLE CAKE.

Make the cake by the same recipe as for orange cake. Bake in three layers.

FILLING.—The whites of two eggs beaten to a stiff froth and a cup of powdered sugar. Grate enough fresh pineapple to have three-quarters of a cup of fruit. Strain, add the juice to the whites of eggs and sugar. Divide it, and into one part add the fruit strained from the juice. Use this for the filling. To the rest beat in half a cup of sugar and half a teaspoonful of almond extract, and ice the top and sides of the cake. It should be done while the cake is hot. This, as well as the orange cake, will keep in tin fresh for a week.

CHOCOLATE LAYER CAKE.

Half a cup of butter, two cups of sugar, three whole eggs, or the whites of six, one cup of milk, three cups of flour, two even teaspoonfuls of cream of tartar and one teaspoonful of soda. Beat butter and sugar to a cream, add the eggs beaten together, sift the cream of tartar and soda in the flour, add the flour alternately with the milk. Bake in four or five layers.

CHOCOLATE FILLING.—Take two unbeaten whites of eggs and a cup and a half of powdered sugar and beat them together. Stir over the fire until smooth and glossy two ounces of Baker's unsweetened chocolate grated, with half a cup of powdered sugar and four tablespoonfuls of boiling water, remove from the fire and stir while hot into the eggs and sugar, and when it is cool spread the top and sides, and set the cake in the oven for a moment to dry the icing.

POOR MAN'S CAKE (a Norwegian Recipe).

Twenty yolks of eggs, five whites of eggs, a pound and a quarter of sugar, one pint of sweet cream or rich milk, a sherry glass of cognac, one cup of melted butter, a little pounded cardamom seed, and enough flour to roll thin. Beat the eggs together until light, add the sugar and beat again, then the cream, cognac and butter. Melt the butter and pour off from the salt. Cinnamon may be used instead of cardamom seed. Roll the dough as thin as paper, cut with a jagging iron in oblong pieces, slit one end with the iron and pass the other end through it. Fry in boiling fat, drain on paper, and when perfectly cold put in a stone jar. These cakes will keep for months.

VENISON CAKES (a Norwegian Recipe).

Six eggs beaten light with three-quarters of a pound of sugar, one cup of sweet cream or rich milk, a pound and a half of flour. When these ingredients are well mixed add four ounces of well washed butter, stir well together. Mix with the flour a little less than an even teaspoonful of ammonia, powdered fine—the cakes will rise better—and flavor with cardamom or cinnamon. Roll the dough with the hands until about the thickness of the little finger, cut in pieces about three inches long—the ends bias—lap them and snip with scissors or a knife around the outside to make points, then fry in boiling fat as crullers. These also keep a long time.

SEED CAKES.

A cup and a half of granulated sugar, a cup and a half of butter, four eggs, one tablespoonful of caraway seed and flour to roll. Beat the butter and sugar to a cream, add the yolks beaten light, then the caraway seed. Beat the whites of eggs to a stiff froth and add alternately with the flour—do not make the dough stiff. Roll thin, cut in small cakes and bake in a quick oven.

DROP CAKES.

A cup of butter, a cup and a half of sugar, four eggs, a pint of flour, a cup of currants, half a cup of sweet milk, a teaspoonful of baking powder. Drop with a teaspoon on greased pans and bake in a quick oven ten minutes.

LEBKUCHEN.

Half a pound of granulated sugar, half a pound of strained honey, half a pound of candied orange peel, half a pound of citron, half a pound of almonds blanched and cut fine, an even teaspoonful of bicarbonate of potash pounded very fine and a sherry glass of rum poured over it twenty-four hours before it is used, an even teaspoonful of cloves, an even teaspoonful of cinnamon, an even teaspoonful of powdered cardamom seed, the rind of half a lemon grated, and two eggs. Put the honey in a saucepan and let it come to a boil, pour it over the sugar in a mixing bowl and stir well, then add the flour, mix thoroughly, and set in a cool place for twenty-four hours. Then cut all the fruit fine and mix with the other ingredients thoroughly, beat the eggs and add to the mixture, put in the rum and potash last, stir well, and let it stand for an hour or two. Roll the dough out about a quarter of an inch thick, cut into cakes about three inches wide and five long, bake in a quick oven ten or fifteen minutes. Do not use more than two ounces of flour in rolling out the cakes. Ice them while hot.

ICING.—Half a pound of sugar and the juice of half a lemon and the same quantity of water as of lemon juice; stir together and spread on very thin.

MACAROONS (a Bavarian Recipe).

Blanch and chop fine half a pound of almonds. Beat the whites of three eggs to a stiff froth, add half a pound of sugar and then the nuts. Drop from a small spoon on paraffine paper on a baking sheet and bake a delicate brown in a cool oven.

CHOCOLATE MACAROONS (a Bavarian Recipe).

Two ounces of almonds chopped fine, the whites of three eggs beaten to a stiff froth, stir in six ounces of sugar and an ounce and a half of grated chocolate, then add the almonds. Bake in a cool oven.

SODA CAKES.

Three egg yolks, a pint and a half of cream, three-quarters of a pound of butter, an even teaspoonful of soda, one pound and a half of sugar, and flour enough to roll. Roll very thin and cut in small cakes; put half a blanched almond in the middle of each. Bake in a slow oven.

WALNUT WAFERS.

Beat two eggs very light and add to them half a pound of brown sugar; beat again and stir in half a cup of flour with a quarter of a teaspoonful of baking powder, a third of a teaspoonful of salt and half a cup of walnut meats slightly chopped. Drop in small spoonfuls on buttered tins, not too close together, and bake brown. The dough should not be too thin; try one or two and if too thin add a very little more flour.

JODE CAKES (a Norwegian Recipe).

Three egg yolks, a pint and a half of cream, three-quarters of a pound of butter, an even teaspoonful of soda, one pound and a half of sugar and flour enough to roll. Roll very thin and cut in small cakes; put half a blanched almond in the middle of each. Bake in a slow oven.

FROSTING.

Three-quarters of a cup of powdered sugar to the white of one egg, flavoring to taste. Beat the white of egg to a stiff froth and turn all the sugar into it; see that the sugar is free from lumps, beat hard and flavor according to the cake.

BOILED ICING.

One cup of granulated sugar, five tablespoonfuls of boiling water, the white of one egg beaten to a stiff froth. Put the sugar and water over the fire and boil until it threads from the spoon; then turn it into the beaten egg, beat briskly for a few minutes, flavor with vanilla, lemon or almond, according to the cake. While the cake is still warm, sprinkle with flour and spread the icing on with a broad knife.

Pies.

PLAIN PASTRY.

Four cups of sifted flour, one cup of butter, a pinch of salt, three heaping teaspoonfuls of granulated sugar, two tablespoonfuls of lemon juice, four tablespoonfuls of ice water and the yolks of two eggs. This quantity will make two pies. Rub the butter, flour, salt and sugar together thoroughly, then add the yolks of eggs, lemon juice and water and work all together into a paste. Put the dough on a pastry board, divide in four equal parts, roll each part the size required for the pie plates.

PUFF PASTE.

One pound of flour, one pound of butter and one cup of ice water. Sift the flour, weigh it and turn into a mixing bowl; pour the water gradually into it, stirring constantly with a spoon; turn the dough out on the pastry board and beat or knead it until it blisters and is so elastic that it can be stretched without tearing. Then set it away on ice. Wash the butter, squeeze out the salt and water and lay it on a plate on ice. Roll the dough as nearly square as possible, lay the butter in the center of it, fold over one side of the paste, then the other, flatten slightly with the rolling pin, fold over the ends of the dough until they meet; turn the dough over and roll twice, fold again and put the paste on the ice; let it remain for twenty minutes. Repeat this twice, allowing the pastry to rest twenty minutes each time. This makes in all six rolls and three times of rolling. Press very lightly with the rolling pin, cut off each time what is needed for a pie or number of patties, that the dough will not be worked over more than is necessary. The trimmings may be used for cheese straws by cutting and sprinkling them with grated Parmesan cheese and a dash of cayenne pepper; or may be baked in crescents for garnishing. In baking, rinse the pans with cold water and brush the pastry over with beaten egg. Make the pastry in a cool room.

TO MAKE ONE SQUASH OR PUMPKIN PIE.

One cup of squash, one egg mixed unbeaten with the squash, a cup and a half of sugar, one milk cracker rolled fine, half a teaspoonful each of ginger, cinnamon and nutmeg, a pinch of salt and a dash of cayenne pepper. After these are well mixed, add half a cup of milk. Bake in either puff or plain paste.

SWEET RISSOLES.

Roll out some puff paste into a thin sheet, cut as many rounds with a large patty cutter as are needed; put a spoonful of any kind of jam, strawberry, raspberry, currant, etc., or mince meat or purée of apples on each, moisten the edges of the pastry with water, fold one-half over the other, making them into half moons, brush with beaten egg and bake in a quick oven. They may be varied by sifting coarse sugar and nuts over them before baking.

RICHMOND MAIDS OF HONOR.

Half a pound of dry curd, commonly called cottage or pot cheese, six ounces of butter, four eggs, a glass of brandy, six ounces of sugar, one white potato, one ounce of sweet almonds chopped fine and a few drops of almond extract, the juice of one and the grated rind of two lemons, and a little nutmeg. Mix the curds and butter together, beat sugar and eggs to a cream, add the potato mashed smooth and fine, the almonds, the grated rind and juice of lemon and the nutmeg; beat well and add to the curds and butter, mix thoroughly and bake in tartlet pans or pie plates lined with puff paste.

CHEESE CAKES.

Put a pint of milk on to boil, beat four eggs light and stir into the milk; when it is a thick curd remove from the fire and when cool mash it very fine, add to it four ounces of bread crumbs. Beat to a cream half a pound of butter and half a pound of sugar, add the curds and bread; beat four eggs until very thick and light and pour them into this mixture; then add gradually one tablespoonful of sherry and one of brandy and one of rose-water, and a teaspoonful of cinnamon, and lastly a quarter of a pound of currants well washed. Line either pie plates or shallow cake pans with puff paste, pour in the mixture and bake in a quick oven. They should be served cold and eaten the day they are baked.

COCOANUT PIE (a Southern Recipe).

One cup of freshly-grated cocoanut, one cup of sugar, three eggs, half a lemon, juice and grated rind, one-half cup of cream, one-half cup of butter and one-half cup of cocoanut milk. Beat butter and sugar to a cream, add other ingredients, the yolks of eggs beaten very light with the cream, the lemon juice and rind and lastly the whites of eggs beaten to a stiff froth. Line a dish with puff paste, pour the mixture in and bake in a moderate oven three-quarters of an hour.

LEMON PIE (a Southern Recipe).

The yolks of four eggs beaten to a cream with one cup of granulated sugar and the grated rind of one lemon. Peel the lemon, removing every particle of white skin, cut into thin slices; have a pie plate lined with puff paste, arrange the slices of lemon on the paste, add enough milk to the eggs and sugar to fill the plate, pour it in, and bake until set. Beat the whites of eggs to a stiff froth, and stir in two large heaping tablespoonfuls of sugar, put on top of the pie and bake a light brown.

MINCE MEAT.

One pound of granulated sugar, one pound of raisins, one pound of currants, half a pound of citron, half a dozen lemons, grated rind and juice, the pulp of eight oranges, the grated rind of three, half a pound of almonds blanched and chopped, three pounds of greenings, after they are pared, cored and chopped fine, three heaping teaspoonfuls of powdered cinnamon, an even teaspoonful of allspice, a quarter of a teaspoonful of cloves, an even teaspoonful of salt, three-quarters of a pound of butter melted, a cup and a half of sherry and a cup of brandy. Seed the raisins and soak them with the currants in just water enough to cover, stew until tender, and add when cold with the water to the other ingredients. Mix thoroughly, stirring in the melted butter at the last. Let it stand for several days. The brandy and wine may be omitted and more lemons and oranges used to flavor it. At each baking it is well to add a little sugar and chopped apple. This will keep all winter or longer in a cool place, if the brandy and wine are not omitted.

Candies.

CHOCOLATE CARAMELS.—No. 1.

Six pounds of light brown sugar, one pound of butter, one pound of chocolate, one pint of cream, one pint of milk, paraffine as large as a walnut, one teaspoonful of cream of tartar. Flavor with vanilla. Put all the ingredients together and boil until it is brittle in water; flavor and pour into buttered tins and mark in squares before it is quite cold.

CHOCOLATE CARAMELS.—No. 2.

One pint of fresh milk, three ounces of chocolate, grated, two pounds of granulated sugar, half a teaspoonful of cream of tartar. Stir until melted, then add half a pint of cream, cook until the mixture is brittle in ice water, then turn into a pan well greased and mark in squares when almost cold.

CHOCOLATE CARAMELS.—No. 3.

A quarter of a pound of chocolate, grated, one large cup of granulated sugar, one cup of milk and a heaping tablespoonful of butter, a quarter of a teaspoonful of cream of tartar. Boil all together, stirring all the time, until the syrup hardens in cold water, and just before taking from the fire add a teaspoonful of vanilla. Beat the syrup as soon as removed from the fire, and keep it up until it is too stiff to beat any longer—if it is beaten a minute and a half it will do well. Turn out of the saucepan into a greased pan and before it is quite cold cut in squares.

CHOCOLATE CREAM PEPPERMINTS.

Mix together two cups of granulated sugar and half a cup of cream, boil until it holds well together in cold water, or can be rolled between the fingers, flavor with oil of peppermint, remove from the fire and stir until the cream is stiff enough to mould into balls. Use powdered sugar on the hands while moulding. Melt an ounce of chocolate and dip the balls, which should be as large as hazel nuts, in this, using a long pin for the purpose, and lay them on paraffine paper. Any flavoring may be used instead of peppermint.

CANDY (to Pull).

Two cupfuls of granulated sugar, half a cup of water, one tablespoonful of vinegar, butter the size of a walnut. Boil the sugar and water without stirring until it is brittle when tried in cold water, add the butter and vinegar just before it is done. Flavor with any extract preferred, pour into buttered soup plates, and when cool enough to handle pull until white.

CHESTNUTS GLACÉ.

Skin the chestnuts and cover with cold water, let them cook gently until tender, when a large needle can be run through them easily. Drain and drop them in cold water. After two hours drain again and put them in a bowl, cover them with a rich syrup that has been skimmed and boiled until clear. It must be boiling when poured over the chestnuts. Cover the bowl with a heavy paper and let it stand for twelve hours, drain off the syrup, bring it to the boiling point and turn it over the chestnuts again and put away for another twelve hours. Repeat this process three times, then drain the syrup off and the chestnuts are ready for use. Use the large imported chestnuts, remove the shells and boil the nuts. The brown skin can then be easily removed with a penknife. They are very nice but very troublesome to prepare.

COCOANUT CAKES.

One pound of granulated sugar, half a pound of grated cocoanut, half a cup of water and a saltspoonful of cream of tartar. Boil the sugar and water together until, when dropped in cold water, it can be rolled between the fingers into a ball. Remove from the fire, stir with a wooden spoon until it becomes white and thick like cream, add the cocoanut, stir well and drop with the spoon on paraffine paper or a tin baking sheet, and form into thin round cakes. Set away to dry.

HOARHOUND CANDY.

Put a tablespoonful of dried hoarhound leaves in a cup and pour over them half a cupful of boiling water, cover and let it steep until cold, strain and pour it over a pound of granulated sugar and a tablespoonful of vinegar. Boil without stirring, and if any scum rises to the top remove it. Test the candy in cold water, when brittle remove from the fire and pour into a buttered pan. Mark into squares before it is cold, or break into irregular pieces.

MARSHMALLOWS.

Powder very fine eight ounces of gum arabic, dissolve it in three gills of water over a slow fire and strain. Simmer an ounce and a half of marshmallow roots in two gills of water, for ten minutes, closely covered. Strain and reduce to one gill. Add this with half a pound of sugar to the dissolved gum. Boil until it becomes a thick paste, stirring constantly. Add the whites of four eggs beaten to a stiff froth and a teaspoonful of vanilla extract. Remove from the fire, pour into a pan dusted thickly with cornstarch and when cool cut into squares with a sharp knife, roll in pulverized sugar and pack in a tin box.

NOUGAT.

A pound of granulated sugar, one teaspoonful of salt, one cup of blanched and finely chopped almonds or peanuts, or it may be made of mixed nuts. Dissolve the sugar in a spider over the fire without water, stirring constantly, and when entirely melted mix in the nuts quickly and pour at once into a well greased pan, and before it is cold mark in squares. This is very nice pounded fine in a mortar or ground in a mill to sprinkle over custards just before serving.

PANOCHE (a Spanish Recipe).

Two cups of dark brown sugar, one cup of chopped walnuts, half a cup of milk, butter the size of a walnut. Cook the sugar and milk together, boiling gently from seven to ten minutes, until, when tried in water, it holds well together, and can be rolled into a soft ball. Remove from the fire. Have the chopped nuts in a large bowl, pour over them a teaspoonful of vanilla extract, pour the candy over them and beat with long, rapid strokes until it begins to thicken—it should be like a cream wafer—turn out on paraffine paper, and break it or cut in pieces.

PEPPERMINT DROPS.

Two cups of granulated sugar, half a cup of cold water, a tiny pinch of cream of tartar. Boil ten minutes without stirring, let the sugar melt slowly that it may not burn. Add eight drops of oil of peppermint while still on the fire. When removed from the stove beat with an egg-beater until it falls in long drops, when drop quickly on paraffine paper.

PRALINES.

Two cups of granulated sugar, one-half cup of water, two cups of pecans, hickory nuts or English walnuts. Put the water and sugar on to boil, let it cook without stirring until it threads, remove from the fire and stir in the nuts until they are sugared. Spread on paraffine paper to cool.

VASSAR FUDGE.

Two cups of sugar, two squares or one ounce of Baker's unsweetened chocolate, a scant cup of milk, one tablespoonful of butter. Boil for ten minutes until it holds well together when dropped in cold water. Take from the fire, flavor with a teaspoonful of vanilla extract, beat from three to five minutes until thick and creamy, turn into a buttered pan and cut in squares.

Preserves.

PRESERVE OF MIXED FRUITS.

Five pounds of ripe currants or cherries, five pounds of granulated sugar, two pounds of seeded raisins, the pulp of six oranges cut in small pieces, and the rind of two oranges cut fine. Boil three-quarters of an hour. Grapes can be used instead of currants or cherries.

RED CURRANT JAM.

Pick the currants from the stems, weigh them, and allow three-quarters of a pound of white sugar to a pound of the fruit. Put the currants in a preserving kettle, mash them a little to prevent them from sticking to the kettle, and boil for fifteen minutes, then add the sugar and boil rapidly for ten minutes. Bottle and seal tight.

RED CURRANT JELLY.

Berries for jelly must be picked when the weather is dry. Pick them over, taking out all leaves, etc., put them in the kettle and mash them a little to get enough juice to keep them from burning; stir constantly, and as soon as hot wring them dry through a cheese cloth. Measure the liquid and to every pint of juice allow one pound of sugar. Put the juice on the fire and boil fifteen minutes, then add the sugar and boil fifteen minutes more, skimming thoroughly. Pour into glasses while hot; let them stand until the next day and cover. Very often jelly is soft, and always from one of two reasons: either the berries have been picked immediately after a rain or the sugar is adulterated.

RED CURRANT SYRUP.

The currants must be fresh and perfectly ripe and picked in dry weather. Wash and put them in either a porcelain-lined or a granite-ware kettle, stir until they are tender, as for currant jelly, then remove from the fire and wring them as dry as possible in a cheese cloth. Measure the juice and return it to the fire, let it cook fifteen minutes, then add a pound of granulated sugar to each quart of juice, boil gently fifteen minutes, skimming as long as the scum rises. Bottle and cork well and keep in a dark place. Raspberry and strawberry syrup are made in the same way, only mashing and straining the fruit and measuring the juice before cooking.

BLACK CURRANT SYRUP.

Pick from the stems and mash them, a few at a time, in a bowl or granite saucepan with a potato masher, then put them in a stone jar and let them stand for two days, stirring well each day. Wring them through a cheese cloth, and if wanted sweet cook with sugar as red currant syrup. The juice can be bottled without sugar or cooking, and will keep for years. It is used for sauces or fruit soups, etc.

CRANBERRY JAM.

Put five quarts of cranberries in a preserving kettle with two quarts of water and boil gently until the fruit is tender, then add three pounds and three-quarters of granulated sugar, boil until the fruit is clear, skimming carefully. Put in glasses and when cold seal. It keeps well.

GOOSEBERRY JELLY.

Use the large English gooseberries and follow directions for currant jelly.

GOOSEBERRY JAM.

Three-quarters of a pound of sugar to every pound of fruit. Put the fruit on by itself in a porcelain-lined or granite-ware saucepan, mash and stir well to keep from burning, and boil one hour. Then add the sugar and boil one hour more.

GRAPE JAM.

Press with the fingers the pulp from grapes—Muscat or Concord grapes make the best jam—seed and measure them, allowing a cup of sugar to each cup of fruit. Put the skins on and cook until tender, when almost done add the pulp, and when all is tender add the sugar and boil until thick.

PINEAPPLE JAM.

Pare the fruit and carefully take out the eyes, then grate it on a coarse grater, rejecting the cores, weigh it, and to each pound of fruit take a pound of sugar. Sprinkle it over the grated pines, let it stand over night. In the morning, boil for ten or fifteen minutes over a quick fire. Put in tumblers and when cold cover.

RASPBERRY OR STRAWBERRY JAM.

Allow three-quarters of a pound of sugar to a pound of fruit. Put the fruit in a preserving kettle over the fire and boil fifteen minutes, mashing a little to prevent sticking to the kettle. Then add the sugar and boil ten minutes, skimming carefully; turn into glasses and seal when cold.

ORANGE MARMALADE.

Select smooth, thin-skinned, juicy oranges. Take twenty-one, and five lemons. Cut the rind very thin from a third of the fruit, and boil it in two quarts of water until it can be pierced easily with a broom straw. Drain from the water and cut in fine strips with scissors, add this to the pulp of the oranges and lemons after removing all the white bitter skin and pips from the fruit. Weigh and allow a pound of sugar to a pound of fruit, put in a porcelain-lined or granite-ware kettle and cook until clear. Put in glasses and when cold cover with brandied paper and seal.

PUMPKIN CHIPS.

Slice very thin and chip about four pounds of pumpkin, put in an earthenware bowl, and cover it over night with four and a half pounds of granulated sugar and the juice of one dozen lemons. Boil the lemon peel until tender and cut in small thin chips and add to the juice, etc. In the morning, boil together until perfectly clear and crisp.

Pickles, Sauces, etc.

RIPE CUCUMBER PICKLE.

Pare and seed the cucumbers. Slice each cucumber lengthwise in four pieces or cut it in fancy shapes, cover with cold vinegar and let them stand for twenty-four hours. Drain and put them in fresh vinegar with two pounds of sugar, and one ounce of cassia buds to one quart of vinegar. Boil for twenty minutes and put in jars.

SWEET PICKLED PEACHES.

Select fine, fresh, ripe, but not soft peaches, peel and weigh them. To every seven pounds of fruit take five pounds of granulated sugar, a pint of vinegar, two tablespoonfuls of cinnamon and one tablespoonful of cloves, tie the spices up in a muslin bag, add a few pieces of stick cinnamon and a few allspice. Put the fruit in a stone jar, bring the sugar, vinegar and spice to a boil, pour over the peaches, cover and let them stand until the next day, scald the syrup again and pour over the fruit, and so on, until it has been done in all seven times. Take out the bag of spice and put the fruit with the syrup into jars and seal. These are much more delicious than peaches that are cooked.

SWEET PICKLED PLUMS.

Follow the recipe for sweet pickled peaches.

SPICED CURRANTS.

Take seven pounds of fresh and perfectly ripe currants, pick them over, wash and stem them and put in a granite-ware or porcelain-lined kettle, with five pounds of granulated sugar, one even tablespoonful of cloves, one tablespoonful of cinnamon, one dessert-spoonful of allspice, one pint of best cider vinegar. Boil an hour and a half, put in jars and when cold seal.

CHILI SAUCE.

Four dozen ripe tomatoes, eight green peppers, three cups of chopped onion, eight cups of cider or wine vinegar, two cups of brown sugar, two tea-spoonfuls of ginger, three teaspoonfuls of cinnamon, two teaspoonfuls of allspice, two teaspoonfuls of cloves, eight tablespoonfuls of salt. Skin the toma-toes and put them in the kettle over the fire; as soon as the water runs from them, take out half of it, then put in the onions and peppers chopped, boil together four hours, stir constantly the last hour to prevent burning, then add the other ingredients and simmer long enough thoroughly to mix them. Put the sauce in small bottles, cork tight and seal and keep in a dark place.

CHILI PEPPER SAUCE.

Twenty ripe tomatoes, six green peppers and four white onions chopped fine, two cups of best wine or cider vinegar, one cup of sugar, two tablespoonfuls of salt, two even teaspoonfuls of ground mace, two teaspoonfuls of nutmeg, two teaspoonfuls of cloves, one teaspoonful of celery seed. Boil an hour and bottle while hot. Very nice to serve with baked beans.

MUSTARD PICKLES.

One quart each of tiny whole cucumbers, large cucumbers sliced, green tomatoes sliced and small button onions, one large cauliflower divided into flowerettes, and four green peppers cut fine. Make a brine of four quarts of water and one pint of salt, pour it over the mixed vegetables and let it stand covered twenty-four hours. Then scald it and turn into a colander to drain. Mix one cup of flour, six tablespoonfuls of mustard, and one tablespoonful of turmeric with enough vinegar to make a smooth paste, add one cup of granulated sugar and sufficient vinegar to make two quarts in all. Boil this mixture until it is thick and smooth, stirring constantly, then add the vegetables and heat them through.

RIPE TOMATO PICKLE.

A peck of perfectly ripe tomatoes, two quarts of fine cooking salt, half a pound of ground mustard, one ounce of cloves, two green peppers, two or three onions and one pound of brown sugar. Pierce the tomatoes with a silver fork or broom straw, put them in a stone jar with salt in alternate layers. Throw away all the liquor made by standing one week. Return to jar and cover with cold water, cover and let it stand twenty-four hours. Drain again thoroughly, throw away the water, return the tomatoes to the jar and cover with cold vinegar, having added to the fruit, the onions and peppers sliced, with the mustard, cloves and sugar. After they have stood three weeks they are ready for use.

GREEN TOMATO PICKLES.

One peck of sliced tomatoes, eight onions, one pound of bell peppers, one pound of horse radish, one pound of white mustard seed, half a pound of black mustard seed, half an ounce of whole cloves, half an ounce of stick cinnamon, half an ounce of pepper corns, one or two nutmegs and four pounds of sugar. Select the tomatoes when they are beginning to turn white, slice and lay them in salt for twenty-four hours. Drain and put in the kettle, which should be of granite ware or porcelain lined, with the peppers, onions and horse radish chopped, and sprinkle the mustard seeds over all. Tie the spices in a thin muslin bag and cover the whole with best wine vinegar, boil until tender and clear in appearance. The peppers should have all the seeds removed. Half a cup of dry mustard is considered by some an improvement.

GOOSEBERRY CATSUP.

Boil ten pounds of large English gooseberries, seven pounds of coffee sugar, and three pints of vinegar together for an hour and a half. Then add two tablespoonfuls of cinnamon, one of allspice and one of cloves and boil half an hour longer. Put in jars and seal.

RASPBERRY VINEGAR.

Put a pound of fine fruit into a bowl and pour over it a quart of the best wine or cider vinegar. Next day strain the liquor on a pound of fresh raspberries. The following day do the same. Do not squeeze the fruit, but drain as dry as possible by lightly pressing it. The last time strain it through muslin previously wet with vinegar to prevent waste. Put into a preserving kettle with a pound of sugar to every pint of juice. Stir until the sugar is melted and let it cook gently for five minutes, skim it. When cold, bottle and cork well.

Sweet Sauces.

FRUIT SAUCE.

Put a cupful of granulated sugar in a saucepan, pour over it two and a half cupfuls of boiling water, let it boil a few minutes, then add two heaping tablespoonfuls of butter, two even teaspoonfuls of cornstarch rubbed to a paste with a little cold water, then add a cupful of canned fruit or a glass of any kind of fruit or jelly liked and the juice of a lemon. Press through a fine sieve and serve with fritters or puddings.

FRESH FRUIT SAUCE.

Follow the above recipe, using a cupful of pure juice of the fruit desired and the juice of either a half or whole lemon.

ORANGE SAUCE.

Beat four egg yolks, three ounces of sugar, a teaspoonful of flour and the grated rind of one orange together until light, add a pint of boiling milk and stir over the fire until thick, taking care that it does not curdle, remove from the fire and add a liqueur glass of curaçoa, and beat until light and foaming.

BANANA SAUCE.

Rub two bananas through a fine sieve. Put half a cup of granulated sugar in a saucepan with one cup of boiling water, add the banana pulp to it, let it come to a boil, and skim if necessary. Rub a heaping tablespoonful of butter with half a tablespoonful of flour, stir into it a little of the liquid, and then add to that in the saucepan; add the juice and grated rind of half a lemon, and it is ready to serve.

FOAMING SAUCE.

Beat to a cream a cup of sugar and a quarter of a cup of butter, and add to it two tablespoonfuls of wine or fruit juice, or in winter fruit syrup. If the latter, use only three-quarters of a cup of sugar. At serving time add a quarter of a cup of boiling water, stir well, then add the white of an egg beaten to a stiff froth. Beat until the sauce foams.

HARD SAUCE.

Cream one tablespoonful of butter, stir in four tablespoonfuls of powdered sugar and beat until very light, then add a teaspoonful of boiling water and beat again. Flavor to suit taste.

SOUTHERN SAUCE.

Beat four tablespoonfuls of brown sugar with two tablespoonfuls of butter to a cream, and add the well-beaten yolks of two eggs, set the bowl in a pan of hot water on the stove and stir until thick, add a glass of sherry, stir well and it is ready to serve.

VANILLA SAUCE.

Put a pint of rich milk in a double boiler, sweeten with two tablespoonfuls of granulated sugar. While the milk is coming to the boiling point beat the yolks of four eggs until light and creamy, add the hot milk to the eggs, stirring briskly, then turn it into the boiler, stirring rapidly until it thickens, remove from the fire, turn into a bowl, flavor with vanilla extract and serve very cold.

SAUCE FOR NOODLE PUDDING.

Four egg yolks, four ounces of sugar, a quarter of a cup of sherry, one teaspoonful of potato flour, half a cup of water, the rind of half and the juice of one lemon. Beat quickly over hot water until the sauce thickens, then serve at once.

MAPLE SYRUP SAUCE.

Half a pound of maple sugar dissolved in half a cup of cream, or rich milk. If the latter is used add a teaspoonful of butter.

Savory Sauces.

In making sauces great care should be taken to have the saucepans scrupulously clean and only granite-ware or porcelain-lined saucepans should be used, especially where there is any acid as in tomatoes or pickles. Never use an iron spider except for browning butter and flour together as they will not brown in a saucepan.

VEGETABLE STOCK FOR SAUCES.

Take any kinds of vegetables convenient, such as parsnips, celery, carrots, turnips, green pepper, onion, leek, parsley, celery tops, celery root, Jerusalem artichokes, a bay leaf, two cloves, two allspice, and cook in water until tender; strain, pressing all from the vegetables. The water Jerusalem artichokes are boiled in is valuable for sauces. The liquid from canned peas is also excellent. Care must be taken in putting the vegetables together not to let any one predominate, turnip especially, as it makes a sauce very bitter.

COLORING FOR SAUCES, SOUPS, Etc.

Melt a quarter of a pound of granulated sugar in a spider, cook until it is a very dark, rich brown, almost black, stir constantly. Great care must be taken that it does not burn. When done pour over it a quart of boiling water and let it cook until the caramel is entirely dissolved, pour it out and when cold strain and bottle. It will keep indefinitely and a tablespoonful will give color to a pint of liquid.

OLIVE SAUCE.

Melt a heaping tablespoonful of butter in a spider and when it begins to brown stir into it a heaping tablespoonful of flour, let it cook until a very dark brown, but be careful not to let it burn, then add enough rich vegetable stock to make a thick cream-like sauce. Have ready some olives—six or seven, that have been boiled a few minutes in water and cut from the stones, add these to the sauce, season with pepper and salt to taste, bring to the boiling point and serve.

SAUCE HOLLANDAISE.

One-quarter of a pound of butter, one-quarter of a cup of water, one-quarter of a teaspoonful of salt, the juice of a quarter of a lemon, a dash of cayenne, and the yolks of three eggs. Beat the butter to a cream and stir in the yolks of eggs, one at a time, then the lemon juice, salt and pepper. Set the bowl it is mixed in in a pan of boiling water on the fire, beating constantly with an egg beater, and when it begins to thicken stir in gradually the boiling water. When it is as thick as soft custard it is done. Great care must be taken not to let it remain too long on the fire or it will curdle.

DRAWN BUTTER OR CREAM SAUCE.

Melt a large heaping tablespoonful of butter and stir into it a heaping teaspoonful of flour, let them cook together without browning and add by degrees a cup of hot milk.

CURRY SAUCE.

Curry sauce is made by adding curry powder to taste to a white sauce. It may likewise be added to a brown sauce.

CHEESE SAUCE.

A white or cream sauce with grated Parmesan cheese added to taste.

TOMATO SAUCE.

Melt a large tablespoonful of butter in a saucepan over the fire, when it bubbles put into it a small onion and half a green pepper, if convenient, chopped very fine. Simmer gently for a few minutes, then stir in a heaping teaspoonful of flour, and add four nice, fresh tomatoes peeled and cut small—canned tomatoes may be used—a gill of vegetable stock, a clove and part of a bay leaf, and pepper and salt to taste. Let it cook gently for half an hour and press through a fine sieve.

SAUCE TARTARE

may be made by beating a small tablespoonful of butter to a cream, adding salt, pepper, dry mustard and sugar to taste and the raw yolk of an egg. Add a tablespoonful of olives, small cucumbers and capers chopped very fine and a few drops of onion juice. Serve with mock fish cutlets and croquettes.

SAUCE PIQUANTE.

Melt a heaping tablespoonful of butter in a spider and when it bubbles stir into it a heaping tablespoonful of flour, cook until it turns a dark brown, taking care not to let it burn, add to it enough well-seasoned vegetable stock to make the sauce the proper consistency, then pour it into a granite-ware saucepan and add one small cucumber pickle, two olives and a few capers, all chopped very fine; season with salt and pepper to taste.

Sandwiches.

CHEESE SANDWICHES.

Half a pound of grated cheese, one tablespoonful of butter, the yolks of two hard-boiled eggs mashed very fine and a teaspoonful of mayonnaise dressing. Mix the ingredients thoroughly; butter before cutting from the loaf some slices of brown or white home-made bread; spread with the mixture and fold together.

CELERY SANDWICHES.

Use dainty little baking powder biscuits freshly baked but cold, or white home-made bread for these sandwiches. Only the very tender part of celery should be used and chopped fine and put in iced water until needed. Add a few chopped walnuts to the celery and enough mayonnaise dressing to hold them together; butter the bread before cutting from the loaf, spread one slice with the mixture and press another over it. If biscuits are used, split and butter them. They should be small and very thin for this purpose and browned delicately.

NUT AND CREAM CHEESE SANDWICHES.

Boston brown bread buttered on the loaf and cut in very thin slices; spread with a filling of cream cheese and chopped walnut meats; press a buttered slice over it. They may be cut in fingers, rounds or half-moons. The proportion is three-quarters of a cup of nuts to a ten-cent package of Philadelphia cream cheese. This quantity will make a large number of sandwiches.

NUT SANDWICHES.

Graham, rye, and Boston brown bread make very nice sandwiches. Butter the loaf and cut in very thin slices, sprinkle with chopped nuts and fold together.

WHOLE WHEAT BREAD AND PEANUT SANDWICHES.

Chop the nuts very fine, butter the bread before cutting from the loaf, sprinkle the nuts thickly over the butter, press two slices together. Boston brown bread with raisins is also nice for these sandwiches.

OLIVE SANDWICHES.

Prepare the bread and butter as for other sandwiches. It may be cut in squares, rounds or triangles to suit the fancy. Stone and chop as many Queen olives as needed and mix with them enough mayonnaise dressing to hold together, spread half the number of bread slices with the mixture and cover with the other half.

Brown, rye, whole wheat or white bread may be used. Home-made is preferable, but it must be twelve hours old. Sandwiches may be sweet or savory, may be cut round, square, or in triangles.

Sundries.

CRACKERS AND CHEESE TOASTED.

Butter some zepherettes and sprinkle thickly with grated Parmesan cheese, bake in a quick oven, or toast on a gridiron; serve hot.

CRACKERS WITH CREAM CHEESE AND GUAVA JELLY.

Spread zepherettes with cream cheese and dot with Guava jelly.

WELSH RAREBIT.

Half a pound of American cheese, two butter balls, two eggs, half a teaspoonful of mustard, a saltspoonful of salt, a dash of cayenne pepper, half a cup of milk and an even saltspoonful of soda. Cut the cheese fine, melt the butter in a chafing dish or spider, stir the mustard, salt and pepper with it, then add the cheese and milk; when the cheese is dissolved add the eggs slightly beaten and stir until it thickens. Serve on toast.

CHEESE SOUFFLÉ.

Melt one tablespoonful of butter in a spider, add to it a slightly heaping tablespoonful of flour and one cup of hot milk, half a teaspoonful of salt, a dash of cayenne pepper and one cup of grated Parmesan cheese; then add the yolks of three eggs beaten light, remove from the fire and let it cool; then add the whites of eggs beaten stiff, turn into a pudding dish, bake twenty-five minutes and serve immediately.

CHEESE STRAWS.

Take two ounces of flour and three ounces of Parmesan cheese grated (it is better to buy the cheese by the pound and have it grated at home), and two ounces of butter. Rub the butter into the flour, add the cheese and a little salt and cayenne pepper, and make into a paste with the yolk of an egg; roll the paste out in a sheet about an eighth of an inch thick and five inches wide and cut in narrow strips; bake in a hot oven about ten minutes.

PÂTE À CHOU FOR SOUPS.

Put a gill of milk and an ounce of butter into a saucepan over the fire; when it comes to the boiling point add two ounces of sifted flour; stir with a wooden spoon until thick and smooth, then add two eggs, one at a time, beating briskly; remove from the fire and spread out thin, cut in pieces, the size of a small bean, put them in a sieve, dredge with flour, shake it well and fry in boiling fat until a nice brown. Add to the soup after it is in the tureen.

A FILLING FOR PATTIES.

Break two eggs in a bowl, add a little salt and white pepper, a few drops of onion juice and four tablespoonfuls of cream, beat slightly; turn into a buttered tin cup, stand in a saucepan with a little boiling water in it on the stove, cover and cook until stiff—about three or four minutes—remove from the fire, turn out of the cup. When ready to use cut in half-inch slices and then into stars or any fancy shape preferred, or into dice. Make a cream sauce thicker than for other uses, that it may not run through the pastry; put them in the sauce, bring to the boiling point and fill the patties just as they are to be served.

GRUEL OF KERNEL FLOUR OR MIDDLINGS.

Put a pint of boiling water in a saucepan over the fire; mix two heaping teaspoonfuls of the flour with a little cold water and stir into the boiling water. Let it boil twenty minutes, add a little cream to it and salt. Very nutritious.

KOUMYSS.

Dissolve a third of a cake of compressed yeast in a little tepid water; take a quart of milk, fresh from the cow, or warmed to blood heat, and add to it a tablespoonful of sugar and the dissolved yeast. Put the mixture immediately in beer bottles with patent stoppers, filling to the neck, and let them stand for twelve hours where bread would be set to rise—that is, in a temperature of 68 or 70 degrees—then stand the bottles upside down on ice until wanted.

HOME-MADE BAKING POWDER.

Procure from a reliable druggist one-half pound of the best bicarbonate of soda, one pound of cream of tartar and one-half pound of Kingsford's corn-starch. Mix thoroughly and sift three times, put up in small tins. The best baking powder.

VANILLA EXTRACT.

One ounce of Mexican vanilla bean, two ounces of loaf sugar, eight ounces of French rose water, twenty-four ounces of alcohol 95 per cent. Cut up the bean and pound with the sugar in a mortar, sift and pound again until all is a fine powder. Mix the alcohol and rose water; put the vanilla in a paper filter, pour over it a little of the liquid at a time until all is used; filter again if not all is dissolved. Paper filters may be obtained at any of the large drug stores. The extract may be darkened by using a little caramel.

VANILLA SUGAR.

Half a pound of loaf sugar, half an ounce of Mexican vanilla beans. Cut the beans very fine, pound in a mortar with the sugar; sift and pound again until all is fine. Bottle and cork tight and keep in a dark place.

SPINACH FOR COLORING.

Pound some spinach in a mortar, adding a little water; squeeze through a cheese cloth, put in a saucepan over the fire, bring to a boil; when it curdles remove from the stove. Strain through a very fine sieve; what remains on the under part of the sieve is the coloring. It is used for coloring pistache ice cream, jellies, etc.

TOMATO PASTE FOR SANDWICHES.

Skin and cut small three large tomatoes, cook until tender and press through a sieve fine enough to retain the seeds; return to the fire, add two ounces of butter, two ounces of grated bread crumbs and two ounces of grated Parmesan cheese. When it boils stir a beaten egg quickly into it, remove at once from the fire. It must not boil after the egg is added, as it will curdle. Turn the mixture into a bowl and when cold, if it is not for immediate use, cover with melted butter.

CHEESE PASTE FOR SANDWICHES.

Boil two eggs hard, separate the yolks from the whites, mash the yolks smooth and chop the whites very fine; mix and put through a vegetable press, then add butter the size of a small egg and three heaping tablespoonfuls of grated American cheese. Beat together until it is a fine, smooth paste. If not salt enough add a little, and also dry mustard, if liked.

Miscellaneous Recipes.

TOOTH POWDER.

Precipitated chalk, seven ounces; Florentine orris, four ounces; bicarbonate of soda, three ounces; powdered white Castile soap, two ounces; thirty drops each of oil of wintergreen and sassafras. Sift all together and keep in a glass jar or tin box. A very valuable recipe for hardening the teeth.

JAPANESE CREAM.

Four ounces of ammonia, four ounces of white Castile soap cut fine, two ounces of alcohol, two ounces of Price's glycerine and two ounces of ether. Put the soap in one quart of water over the fire; when dissolved add four quarts of water; when cold add the other ingredients, bottle and cork tight. It will keep indefinitely. It should be made of soft water or rain water. To wash woolens, flannels, etc., take a teacup of the liquid to a pail of lukewarm water, and rinse in another pail of water with half a cup of the cream. Iron while damp on the wrong side. For removing grass stains, paint, etc., use half water and half cream.

ORANGE FLOWER LOTION FOR THE COMPLEXION.

Dissolve a slightly heaping tablespoonful of Epsom salts in a pint of imported orange flower water (Chiris de Grasse), and add to it one tablespoonful of witch hazel. Apply with a soft linen cloth. Very refreshing in warm weather and an excellent remedy for oiliness of the skin.

BAY RUM.

Three-quarters of an ounce of oil of bay, one ounce of loaf sugar, one pint of alcohol, 95 per cent., two quarts of new New England rum and three pints of rectified spirits, 60 per cent. Roll the sugar until fine and beat into the oil of bay, add the alcohol, then the New England rum and spirits. Let it stand for several days in a demijohn, shaking occasionally; then filter through blotting paper. The filters may be purchased at a druggist's. Care should be taken to buy the oil at a reliable place.

FINE LAVENDER WATER.

Two ounces finest oil of lavender, one ounce essence of musk, one-half ounce essence of ambergris, one-half ounce oil of bergamot and one-half gallon of rectified spirits. Mix the ingredients, keep in a demijohn for several days, shaking occasionally. Then filter and bottle.

GOOD HARD SOAP.

Five pounds of grease, one quart and one cup of cold water, one can of potash, one heaping table-spoonful of borax, two tablespoonfuls of ammonia. Dissolve the potash in the water, then add the borax and ammonia and stir in the lukewarm grease slowly and continue to stir until it becomes as thick as thick honey; then pour into a pan to harden. When firm cut into cakes. Grease that is no longer fit to fry in is used for this soap. Strain it carefully that no particles of food are left in it. It makes no difference how brown the grease is, the soap will become white and float in water. It should be kept a month before using.

POLISH FOR HARD OR STAINED WOOD FLOORS.

Eight ounces of yellow beeswax, two quarts of spirits of turpentine, one quart of Venetian turpentine. Cut the wax in small pieces and pour the spirits over it—it will soon dissolve; then bottle. Apply with a flannel or soft cloth. It keeps the floors in excellent order.

CONTENTS.

BREADS, ROLLS, Etc.

EGGS.

ENTRÉES.

VEGETABLES.

SALADS.

FRUIT DESSERTS.

DESSERTS. PUDDINGS.

ICE CREAMS AND WATER ICES.

CAKES.

MISCELLANEOUS RECIPES.

MISCELLANEOUS RECIPES.

www.ingramcontent.com/pod-product-compliance
Lightning Source LLC
Chambersburg PA
CBHW020539270326
41927CB00006B/644